Bob Lancer's
Parenting With Love
Without Anger Or Stress

2007 Revised Edition

Bob Lancer's
Parenting With Love
Without Anger Or Stress
2007 Revised Edition

Published by
GDG Publishing, LLC
Atlanta, GA
www.GDGPublishing.com

ISBN: 0-9796625-8-3; 978-0-9796625-8-4

Library of Congress Cataloging-in-Publication Data
available upon request.

First Edition publication date: 1997,
with subsequent reprinting in
1999, 2001, 2003, 2005

Visit gdgpublishing.com or boblancer.com for a complete listing of Bob Lancer's
books, recordings and information about Bob Lancer's seminars and keynotes.

I Humbly Dedicate This Book
To The Sacred Heart Of Every Child

Acknowledgements:
Cover Design: Richard Heiman

Essential influences include:
Isidore Friedman
Alfred Korzybski
Maria Montessori
Alice Miller

Bob Lancer's
Parenting With Love
Without Anger Or Stress
TABLE OF CONTENTS

PART FOUR: YOUR CHILD DISCIPLINE OPTIONS

PART FIVE: PRIMARY PARENTING SOLUTIONS

PART SIX: SECONDARY PARENTING SOLUTIONS

"...come mothers and fathers throughout the land
and don't criticize what you can't understand
your sons and your daughters are beyond your command..."

Bob Dylan

Introduction
Take Charge Now!

This book teaches you how to be effectively in charge with love, without anger or stress, in your relationship with your child of any age.

When I say "in charge" I do not mean dominating your child in an inflexible, condescending, or bossy manner. I mean relating with your child in a healthy, natural, harmonious way that truly works for both you *and* your child. The approach to parenting that you will learn here neither makes parenting all about your child or all about you. You both count. You are both human beings with a sacred heart. You need to be in charge because you have more experience and competence. But you also need to allow your child to run her own life, to make some mistakes, and to express her authentic self.

You will learn in these pages how to maintain your calm, confident composure as you *competently* fulfill – and even enjoy - even the most rigorous demands of parenting. You will learn how to better meet your child's needs as you meet your own needs for a sane, orderly, balanced life. This book reveals how parents unwittingly cause much of the difficulty they experience in parenting and how you can apply that understanding to ensure that you and your child feel happy, loved, secure, and respected as you *both* demonstrate your finest behavior. You will learn that taking charge of children begins with taking charge of ourselves first, just as taking care of children begins with taking care of ourselves first.

Who This Book Is For

This book is for parents of children of all ages. including those with their first child on the way. It is for parents of children classified as normal, gifted, difficult, and special needs, including children diagnosed with A.D.H.D. It is for the parent of the child in or out of trouble, be that trouble serious or slight. Teachers and caregivers can apply the material here to enjoy greater results more easily with the children they serve. In fact, it is my hope that all adults read this book to better understand and deal with the impact of the parenting they themselves received, as well as to better grasp what children need from all of us to fulfill their glorious potential.

The Real World Of Parenting

When you pay close enough attention, you receive three important insights that operate as the crux of a major aspect of this book's approach to parenting:

Everything you say, think, feel, and do produces some kind of an effect upon you and your child.

We often blame our children for the stressful, dissatisfying ways *that we attempt to manage them.*

Making our child responsible for our reactions makes us feel powerless and victimized by the child.

You can more effectively guide your child's behavior as you replace your frustration and impatience with peace and poise. Without losing your temper, screaming, nagging, pleading, hitting or timing your child out on a routine basis you can achieve more parenting success with more love and ease. You don't have to rush through your day, constantly urge your child to "hurry up," or drag yourself through the valley of fatigue in order to be a responsible parent. You can capably *and calmly* lead your child into the fulfillment of her glorious potential and out of whining, ignoring directions, nagging, arguing, helplessness, tantrums, disrespect, apparent apathy, and aggressiveness. This book shows you how.

In the pages that follow, you will learn ways to make typical "trouble spots" such as bedtime, mealtime, leaving punctually in the morning, and doing homework into smoothly flowing, stress-free routines. You will learn how to effectively establish boundaries that help your child behave responsibly without resorting to draining, self-demeaning power struggles.

It's Time For You To Grow

If this book has one overarching theme, it is this: You can better direct your child as you focus on improving your self-direction. A child's arrival into your life means it's time for *you* to grow, because it brings responsibilities and opportunities that call upon your greater potential. As in every other area of your life, your continuing dedication to the fulfillment of your own higher potential is what it takes to achieve the best results in parenting.

It Doesn't Need To Be That Hard

A while back, a TV news show did a special report on my *Take Charge Now! Parenting With Love Workshop For Parents, Teachers And Childcare Professionals.* The reporter dubbed me "The Guru of Parent Temper Control" because I show how to apply self-control for better child discipline since *you cannot instill greater self-control in a child while you are losing yours.* Reacting with stressful, negative emotion to your child's behavior does not mean that your child is a problem. It means you are working way too hard and treating yourself with too little respect. One of the major themes of my workshop, and of this book, focuses on how to be more effective with less effort.

The Structure Of This Book

Feel free to skip to any part of this book that seems to best suit your present need, but definitely go through this book in its entirety to gain an overall understanding of how your child "works" and how you can work best with him.

Part 1 deals with the start to positive child discipline: parent *self-discipline.* In it you will learn how to take charge of yourself to achieve the results you want through a patient, positive approach to handling every parenting challenge.

Part 2 focuses on the factors that shape your child's personality traits and behavior. It teaches you how to avoid contributing to behaviors and attitudes you do not want and how to support the formation of the ones that you do want.

Part 3 will help you take full advantage of the opportunities of your child's present stage of development. It will also prepare you to handle what comes next and help you to prepare your child to succeed at each future stage of life.

Part 4 teaches you a simple disciplinary system for ending unwanted behavior and promoting responsible behavior without anger or stress.

Part 5&6 provides you with simple, tested parenting solutions. These apply the disciplinary system presented in Part 4 to everyday child behavior challenges, including problems with bedtime, mealtime, lying, sibling rivalry and more. You will also find here some basic guidelines for dealing with single parenting, step parenting, parenting through divorce, grandparenting, and how to relate with your spouse for positive child behavior.

It's About Response-Ability

However your child behaves, as a parent you have responsibility for responding in ways that avoid pushing him into more serious behavior problems; to instead lead him into a higher level of responsible self-direction. That is what I mean by being "in charge." How to accomplish this with peace, love, respect, and joy (for both you and your child) and without unhappiness, debilitating conflict, anger, or stress is what this book is all about. Begin taking charge right now by sincerely deciding to handle every parenting challenge a little more calmly and confidently, with a little more peace and love in your heart and a little less anger and stress. Then, reject any doubt about your ability to do so.

PARENTING WITH LOVE

Is about raising our children
From faith instead of fear,
From love instead of anger,
From strength and tenderness,
From peace instead of strife,
From intention without tension,
From patience, not rush,
From an alert state of consciousness
Focused on the present,
From sane response-ability in place of crazed habitual reaction,
From understanding and parent education,
Instead of ignorance,
With sensitivity and skill, as opposed to brute force,
From respect and kindness,
With an absolute commitment
To enjoying every precious moment
We have with our sacred gift of love, our child.

-Bob Lancer

I

PART ONE

WHERE TAKING CHARGE
WITH LOVE BEGINS

Chapter 1
Peace, Poise And Power

Taking charge in your relationship with your child begins with taking charge of yourself *first*. If your child's behavior drives you crazy, he is in "the driver's seat," and not in a good way. You don't improve your parenting skill by reacting with frustration, annoyance, impatience, and disappointment. These painful conditions make you *out* of control of both yourself and your child. They also make you feel like a victim of your child's behavior. The way to place yourself in charge begins when you accept that your reactions to your child's actions have *nothing* to do with your child's behavior and *everything* to do with how *you* react to it.

Lose Your Peace, Lose Your Power

When you lose your peace and poise (your calm, confident emotional equanimity), you lose your power. It's that simple. The more you react with anger and stress to control your child, the more out of control you and your child become. Angry, stressful reactions might *seem* to achieve for you a momentary semblance of control, but they actually drive a child toward more disturbing behaviors. A parent's show of aggravation inadvertently rewards the child with a negative sense of power that reinforces the child's motivation to continue behaving in an aggravating way. As long as a child can drag you into nagging, pleading, complaining, harshly criticizing, arguing, screaming or even sighing in overwhelm, you place yourself in a weak, dependent position and place that child in charge in a way that serves neither of you.

Ending Of A Myth

We used to believe that reacting to a child with anger and stress was the right, necessary, and responsible way to deal with a disturbing behavior. Now we know that it leads a child toward even more disturbing behavior. You might believe that you are better off because your parents got angry with you. You might believe that your fear of their wrath helped you turn out to be a more responsible adult. The fact is, however, that your parents' display of anger most likely lies at the root of your destructive displays of anger, not your constructive, responsible conduct.

The old myth was based on the assumption that peacefulness equals passiveness, but not necessarily. What you are about to learn here is how to be peaceful *in action* to provide your child with the best influences possible for you.

Angry Reactions Waste Time

As long as you feel angry or stressed, you are prone to relate more destructively with your child. You cannot function at your best - and therefore you cannot produce the best results - when you feel poorly within. You function best when you feel calm and confident. In peace and poise you most skillfully execute. When you feel anger or stress, it is best to give yourself a time out and wait until you regain your composure to deal with what disturbed you. So, ironically, remaining grounded in patience produces more rapid improvement than working with impatience.

Your Peace Radiates

Like the warmth of the sun radiates and warms all within its reach, your inner peace and poise radiate from you and are absorbed by all around you. Thus, the calmer you feel around your child, the more of a calming influence you have upon your child. As you center yourself in peace and poise, your child receives your centering influence and thus exhibits more composure herself. Children behave more cooperatively when they feel calm than when they feel anxious, nervous, or angry. Go into peace and poise, not anger and stress, when you want your child to settle down.

Peace Solves Problems

Your feelings of anger and stress also radiate. In situations where you feel nervous about how your child *might* behave, your nervousness stimulates your child's nervousness, inciting more disruptive behavior from him. By remaining calm in this instance, you avoid triggering what you hope to avoid.

Peace and poise occasionally solve a problem with no need for additional action. For instance, sometimes a child acts out just to get a rise from you. By preserving your peace and poise he receives no incentive to pursue this path of emotional manipulation.

Bear in mind also that calm is healthier than stress, so you literally make yourself sick (or sicker) by reacting stressfully. Since the stress you feel around your child radiates and "soaks into" your child, your stress therefore sickens your child.

Contending With The Hyperactive Child

While all children behave more disruptively under the influence of parental anger and stress, practicing peace and poise around hyperactive children proves especially beneficial, as your calm self-control helps the child to demonstrate more calm self-control. (In twenty-five years of working with children and adults, I have yet to see a hyperactive child without at least one hyper adult at home.)

Bear in mind that your child's feelings also radiate, so that the "hyper radiance" of the hyperactive child may "seep into" the adult to trigger anxious and aggressive reactions. By practicing maintaining your peace and poise under any and all circumstances to the best of your ability, you can develop your power to preserve your peace and poise to the point that it becomes stronger than your child's power to disturb it.

It's Realistic And Idealistic

Parenting peacefully may seem idealistic but it is also the most practical thing in the world. Expecting to improve any situation with anger and stress demonstrates wild idealism because it will never work.

A major cause of reacting with anger and stress can be traced to the false belief that you have to control your child *right now*. When you believe this, your emotional reaction has you duped. If you calm down and observe the situation more patiently, you realize that the world will not come to an end, you can take more time and handle the situation more effectively by handling it more gracefully. What you can do in peace *is* good enough.

How To Take Control

As has been said, peaceful parenting, as I mean it here, is not the same as passive parenting. It is about doing your very best in peace. When you drive yourself so hard that you lose your peace, your efforts surely backfire.

There will be times when it takes all of your strength to remain calm. There will be times when you do not have the strength to control your child *and* maintain your emotional equanimity – your peace and poise – at the same time. In such instances you may have to let your child do as he pleases for a while. But you bring order into a chaotic situation only by working in a calm, orderly manner upon that situation. In peace and poise you can come up with more loving and effective choices and execute those choices more skillfully and successfully. Self-control is your essential foundation for taking constructive control of any situation.

To Grow More Peacefully Effective

To develop your power to parent in peace and poise take 100% responsibility for maintaining your peace and poise. When you blame your child as the cause of your angry, anxious, disturbed reaction, you give your child the power to "make" you react that way and lose your power to preserve your peace.

Make a list of the ways your child behaves that trigger your unhappiness, anger, or stress. Perhaps it happens when she gives you orders in a bossy tone, when she cries and nothing you do soothes or quiets her, when she stalls, whines, nags or deliberately does the opposite of what you know she knows you expect from her. Then view this list and commit yourself to practice handling each of these situations more calmly the next time they, or something similar, occur.

It will be of immeasurable help to routinely visualize yourself peacefully parenting. Try that now. Close your eyes for a few moments and simply imagine yourself parenting with peace and poise. Notice how that feels, how your face looks, how you hold your body. It has been proven time and again that visualizing one-self doing something makes it easier to do. Practice this visualization exercise every morning when you first awaken and every evening before drifting off to sleep.

Your power to remain peaceful grows like the strength of any muscle. Throughout daily living, *practice* handling *everything* with a little more peace and poise. You will find, over time, that little by little you can bring more peace and poise into your responses, making even the most challenging child behavior easier for you to handle.

Monitor Your Feelings

Practice paying close attention to how you feel at all times, particularly in the vicinity of your child. The moment you notice yourself losing peace and poise, stop struggling for so much control and concentrate instead on relaxing into self-control. Take a few deep, calming breaths. Survey your body and relax any tension you might notice in your neck, jaws and shoulders. Relax your face. Slow your pace. Imagine the feeling of peace in your heart. Take a break from worry.

Use This Visual Reminder

To further assist you in remembering to practice peace and poise, draw the following diagram on the back of an index card or an old business card and carry it with you everywhere:

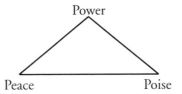

Create several of these diagrams and post them in places where you frequently glance, like the dashboard of your car, the mirror of your bathroom, a cabinet in your kitchen, beside your computer. Every moment that you view it, you strengthen your resolve to maintain peace and poise as your key to real power. It might further assist you to repeat the words, "Peace, Poise, Power," silently to yourself to help you to feel more peace when you need it.

Be Patient With Peace

If you cannot feel perfect peace in an instant, *don't stress about it*. Liberation from habitual stress patterns can be successfully accomplished only by small degrees at a time. Peaceful parenting may be one of the greatest challenges you ever take on in life; it may also be among the most important.

Chapter 2
Conscious Parenting

Conscious Parenting means paying close attention to yourself, your child and the relationship between the two of you *in the present moment* rather than parenting from a habitual mode of automatic, pre-programmed action and reaction. Practicing it consistently will disclose your own way to greater parenting success and satisfaction every single day. In fact, by becoming a more conscious parent – and please read this *consciously* – virtually every one of your frustrations will gradually pass away as you discover easier ways of relating with your child for the results you truly want.

Three Essential Factors

Everything you say, think, feel, and do impacts you, your child and the quality of your relationship. Arguing with your child, for instance, stresses you out, causes your child to feel more stressful and combative, and sends the relationship between you into one of contention and aggression. Even harboring resentful thoughts toward your child causes your child to feel resentful and distrustful and sends the relationship in the direction of mutual enmity, even if that takes place on a subtle level. To accurately sense your impact and to effectively direct your influence, practice closely observing these three factors in the present moment: yourself, your child, and the quality of the relationship between you.

What You Will See

While paying deliberate attention to yourself as you attempt to get your child dressed in the morning, for instance, you might notice that you feel a rise in your tensions. Shifting attention to your child would then reveal that he appears more tense and resistant in response. Observing the quality of your relationship you would notice it heading from harmonious interaction into stiffening opposition. All of this occurs very quickly and subtly. The more you practice Conscious Parenting, the more obvious these subtle shifts become and the more quickly and easily you can improve developments.

In this instance, you would stop struggling to dress your child and instead return to your peace and poise. That shift in itself restores the harmonious feelings between you, and in a harmonious relationship, both individuals are more considerate of one another's feelings and more willing to cooperate with one another. In peace and poise you can come up with more creative, positive solutions that lead your child to get dressed relatively quickly and easily.

The More Aware, The More Control

The biggest obstacle to the deliberate practice of Conscious Parenting is the assumption that you are already as aware as you need to be or as aware as you can be. The fact is that you can always grow more aware through the practice of paying deliberate, focused attention to what is going on between you and your child in the present moment. The effort this takes is well worth it because the more aware you are, the more opportunity you will see and the more pitfalls you will avoid. Practicing Conscious Parenting allows you to recognize the results you are achieving more quickly, so you can change your course for improved outcomes. Your level of awareness equates with your level of control.

Unconscious Parenting

The opposite of Conscious Parenting is Unconscious Parenting. We can describe this as somnambulistic parenting or parenting on "automatic pilot." You do this when you interact with your child habitually, allowing your automatic feeling, action, speech and thought patterns to run you. This compares to driving your car in such a habitual mode that you ignore the unexpected changes in the road.

Your child is always showing you how to win with her, and how to lose, but you have to pay very close attention to recognize the signs.

Awareness Takes Work

To practice Conscious Parenting takes work. You must deliberately practice parenting more consciously to grow into a more conscious—and therefore more capable—parent. Daily review can help you here. Each day, review the times you spent with your child. Just observe the scene as a bystander to see how you handled it and the results you achieved. This daily exercise will make you more aware the following day.

Conscious Parenting is an aspect of *conscious living*. The practice of being more aware of what is going on in the present moment even when you are not with your child will make you more aware when you and your child spend time together.

The Law Of Three

So powerful is this principle of paying conscious attention to the three basic factors of your relationship with your child, that we can call it a law, *The Law of Three*, a term coined by the individual who introduced me to this concept of consciousness, the late Isidore Friedman.

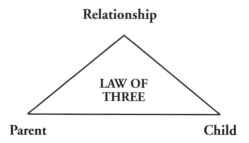

The Law of Three states that you, your child, and the relationship between you are integrally connected and form one whole. Focusing exclusively on yourself or on your child blinds you to the reality of your true impact on all three. Use the diagram on page 17 to assist you in remembering to practice more Conscious Parenting every moment. Let it remind you to look for how your feeling, action, speech and thought influence all three factors in the now. Draw this diagram on an index card and carry it with you, just as you did with your *Peace-Poise-Power* card. Actually hold The Law of Three card in your hand while interacting with your child to help you to remain more vigilant.

An Added Benefit

Just as your level of peace and poise radiates and is absorbed by the child in your vicinity, as we discussed in the previous chapter, so does your level of awareness. Therefore, the more aware you are with your child, the more aware your child will be. Thus, as you practice remaining more aware with your child, your child will automatically exhibit more conscious and conscientious modes of self-conduct.

Chapter 3
A Better Way To Win With Your Child

"Insanity is doing the same thing and expecting different results."
Ancient Chinese Proverb

A better way to win with your child *always* exists. Equally important, it exists within your reach. You can always improve your approach *to some degree* and, as you make even the smallest adjustments, you make it possible to improve your results.

The primary, if not the sole, obstacle to your finding better ways to win with your child is presuming that you are doing all you can do and your child is not doing enough. To do something different does not mean doing more. It may, in fact, entail doing less. But as long as you blame your child for the dissatisfying results you achieve, as long as you presume that you have exhausted all your reasonable options, you prevent yourself from finding a better way and achieving more satisfying results.

What Winning Really Means

To truly *win* with your child means there are no losers. No sane parent can feel like a winner by making his child look, feel, think, or act like a loser. And yet, when a parent slips into an adversarial mindset (or *heartset*) regarding his child, he may blindly seek to make his child feel defeated, outdone, inadequate for his own pleasure of feeling superior, in charge, on top for the moment. This, however, drives a child to do worse, not better. To truly win with your child means winning *for* your child, winning in a way that helps your child win at life.

What Price Are You Willing To Pay?

Parents set themselves and their children up for failure by defining parenting success too narrowly. If winning means nothing more to you than getting your child to do what you want when you want it done you no doubt work way too hard to achieve that short-term *and short-sighted* objective, needlessly hurting yourself and your child in the process. In other words, getting your child to immediately match your expectations may actually be *too* important to you, to the point that you cause you and your child needless suffering.

When you fight your child to, say, put his things away, you turn your home into a war zone. In the trance of an emotional reaction, you might believe that you absolutely *must* get your child to do as you say *this instant.* But don't you *really* need to weigh that against the value of preserving the peace and harmony in your home? When you calmly think about it, which of these two goals truly is more important to you? Which is of greater benefit to your child? This does not mean that you need to endlessly tolerate your child's behavior. It means dedicating yourself to finding *better* ways of winning.

"But He Will Think He's Won!"

Before you can employ a new way of parenting, you need to courageously release yourself from your automatic parenting reaction and accept an uncomfortable period of uncertainty. You have to stop doing what is not working before you can come up with another approach. Therefore, *for the time being,* your child appears to get away with whatever he just did.

At my workshops, a parent occasionally protests against this approach by saying something like, "But if I don't control the situation *immediately,* my child will think that he has won!" As if a child feeling like a winner is a bad thing. I know that's not exactly what the parent really means. But on an unconscious level that is part of what is going on. The parent has fallen into a competitive mindset, which, inevitably, sets parent and child on an increasingly adversarial track. Sure you want cooperation and respect, and you would love to have it happen fast. But do you really want your child's immediate compliance *at all costs?*

To Fight Is Not To Right

To *fight* your child is not to *right* your child. It is to wrong you both, in just about every case. Fighting stresses you out and wears you down, making you less healthy and less capable for less satisfying results. When fighting fills the home, the morale of every household member goes down, lowering the performance level of every family member. The example you set when you bicker with your child teaches your child to bicker. To achieve the best possible results in the most satisfying way, you need to consider all of these factors. In the heat of the moment, you believe that nothing else matters but getting your way right now, but in the clearer light of peace and poise you might realize that nothing could matter less.

Feeling Good Matters

For a child and an adult to demonstrate their finest behavior, both need to feel calm, secure, happy and loved. When your child does not immediately do as you want, maybe she actually needs more freedom in that instance than you realized. Although it does not match your expectations, maybe *this time* you ought to let her walk away from a mess she just made. Maybe *this time* you ought to overlook the fact that she just spit out her food at the table. We need to consider the child's behavior in a larger context than our immediate emotional reaction dictates. For instance, a child grieving over the loss of a loved one may do better if you let her walk away from her mess rather than forcing her to put away her things.

You Produce Your Results

In guiding child behavior, as in every other area of life, what you achieve depends upon what you do. Your child responds to everything you say, think, feel, and do. If you do not believe this, practice Conscious Parenting more consistently. Until you change what *you* do, you cannot improve upon your results with your child. When we ignore this perhaps all too obvious principle, we continue re-creating frustrating scenarios and feel more hopeless and helpless. A better way to win with your child *and for your child* always exists, but you cannot find it as long as you remain stuck in repeating habitual responses.

Where To Begin

Improving your results with your child begins with no longer blaming your child when you get frustrated. When you do not like the results you are getting, instead of complaining in exasperation or pressing on with more intensity, ease up and try a slight shift in your approach. Try lowering your voice instead of raising it. Try giving your child a hug instead of a harsh word. Consider overlooking the behavior instead of dealing with it *right now.* If what you try does not work, don't take it personally. Take it *educationally* and simply try another slight change. If you have no idea what else to do, do nothing for a while but stay calm, pay attention, and remain open to the arrival of a new idea.

Seek And You Will Find

Regard anything you try as an experiment, and regard your results as an education. If something works, continue to use it. If it doesn't work, let it go and try another approach. It works to the extent that you feel happy, at peace, and in love. It needs improvement to the extent that you feel angry and frustrated. It works to the extent that your child feels calm, loving and secure. It works to the extent that it results in your child's responsible behavior. As in every other area of life, you can only achieve greater success in parenting by degrees. If you achieve no other improvement than a reduction of your stress and strain, you have made progress. Continue seeking ways to achieve better and better results and you will find them.

Chapter 4
Choosing The Right Response

Think of your reactions to your child's behavior as a cause rather than as an effect. That single, simple shift in your thinking can make all the difference. Look for how your reactions to your child's actions determine, or at least contribute to, the behaviors your child displays. You might then notice, for instance, that expressing much annoyance when your child makes a grating sound to get your attention actually encourages her to use that tactic again *because it got your attention.*

Before you do something in response to your child's behavior, it helps immeasurably to know *what* to do. You do not want to just do *something.* You want to do the *right* thing. You want to do what *works.*

Misguiding Emotion

To do what works you need to align your response with the outcome you intend. In the grips of an emotional reaction, this becomes nearly impossible. For instance, if your child spills glue on the new carpet, your emotional reaction may tell you to harshly criticize and complain. But all that would end up doing is to make your child feel hurt and angry, perhaps to the point of driving her to seek ways to retaliate rather than show more respect for what you care about. It may also end up undermining her self-confidence, making her more prone to err. It also worsens the quality of your relationship, which further lowers her level of morale and general performance. Thus, your emotional reaction undermines your objective.

Rationalization Protects The Problem

You can easily rationalize that your child deserves to be yelled at for being so careless. But all that does is defend your destructive reaction. You might argue that your child's behavior produces your anger and stress, but that exemplifies just another rationalization that keeps you doing what does not work. The fact is that *you* are totally responsible for how you react and you bear the responsibility for the way that your reaction impacts your child. By discarding rationalizations that support your destructive reactions you make yourself available to more constructive responses.

Let Your Child's Feelings Guide You

When a human being feels hurt, angry, unimportant, disapproved of, antagonized or unsafe (physically or emotionally) he *must* express it through some form of destructive behavior. To direct and to correct your child *correctly,* pay close attention to the physical signs that tell you how he feels. Look for positive, loving ways of guiding your child's behavior so that 95% of the time you spend together is time you both enjoy.

You have the best impact on your child's feelings by feeling really good inside yourself. When you feel calm, loving, secure and content, your child behaves best *because your feeling-state fosters similarly positive feelings in your child.* Choosing the right response therefore involves you handling what happens while feeling calm, caring, content and secure.

Once again, this points to the importance of the practice of handling every behavioral challenge with loving peace and poise. Choosing the right response means choosing to feel calm confidence even when it seems that you have no control over your child. Your harmonious inner feeling state provides essential support for your child's best behavior.

From Knowing To Doing

Another requirement for choosing the right response entails you knowing what it is that you want your response to accomplish. Take some time every day to contemplate deeply what you most truly want for your child, including what sort of parent you want to be for your child. This deepens your awareness of your authentic, core values and liberates you from the misguidance of superficial emotional reactions.

Thinking about what you really want naturally aligns your thoughts, feelings, speech, and actions with your deepest values and intentions, so that you find yourself automatically responding more in line with what you want, instead of emotionally reacting for more frustrating and disappointing results.

Get To Know Your Child Better

Choosing the right response to your child also requires you to have an accurate understanding of your child. One challenge to this is that a child is constantly changing, so you need to pay close attention in the present moment to match your response to your child for the results you truly want. To increase your understanding of your child, spend time everyday just observing your child with an open mind. Try to recognize strengths, weakness, abilities and interests as they emerge. This will help you to better match your responses in any given moment to what will work best with your child.

Parent Your Way

The automatic reaction patterns you learned from your own parents probably represent the biggest obstacle to your correct parenting response. Through repeated exposure to your parents' patterns, you adopted those patterns as your own, just as you adopted your parents' language and other personality characteristics. One problem with doing unto your child as was done unto you is that your child may do much better receiving a very different response from you. Additionally, your parents' patterns might be wrong for *you*, burdening you with excessive stress and strain.

To parent in a way that truly works for the unique self that is you and the unique self that is your child in any given instance, get into deeper touch with your own authentic intentions for your child and pay closer attention to get to know your child more deeply. Then the power of your intention and attention will override the dictate of pre-programmed, unconscious reaction patterns that mismatch the situation.

The F.A.S.T. Formula™

The following diagram illustrates the alignment of your responses with your goals for the most consistent progress toward those goals.

The F.A.S.T. Formula™

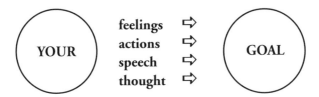

The diagram illustrates the alignment of your four basic levels of response to your child:

Level 1 *Feelings*: your emotional state and attitude

Level 2 *Actions*: what you do physically; the actions you take and how you take them

Level 3 *Speech*: what you say and how you say it

Level 4 *Thought*: the way you think, including the mental visions, expectations and opinions of your child that you hold in your mind

Through each of these levels you impact your child and influence her behavior. To make the most of that influence, align the power of your *feelings* (F), *actions* (A), *speech* (S) and *thought* (T) with your parenting goals. Contemplating your goals or deepest intentions, observing your child, and viewing *The F.A.S.T. Formula*™ diagram on a daily basis will help you to choose responses on all four levels that best align with the outcomes you truly want.

A Tool For Direction

As you look at the diagram, reflect on a past experience you had with your child. Let the diagram assist you in recognizing how well or poorly your responses aligned with your objectives, so that you can make adjustments and respond with better "aim" in the future.

For instance, when your child said that he did not want to go to school this morning:

- How did you *feel?* Did you feel nervous, upset, anxious, insecure, out of control? Those feelings certainly do not help.
- Then look at how you *acted.* Perhaps you handled it better on this level. You may have found a way to get him ready for school by turning it into a game that he chose to participate in. Or maybe you informed him calmly but firmly that if he did not get ready right now on his own he would forfeit his privilege of riding his new bike later in the day, and it worked.
- How did you *speak?* Did you whine, nag, criticize, complain, argue or raise your voice?
- And finally, what were you *thinking?* Were you even conscious enough of your thoughts to remember?

Using the *F.A.S.T.* diagram can also help you in the present. As you did with the previous diagrams, copy this one and carry it with you, viewing it from time to time. Let it remind you, particularly when you feel challenged, that your primary responsibility lies in responding in a way that contributes to the outcome you want, and to avoid responding in ways that work against you and your child.

Chapter 5
Your S.E.A.T. Of Authority

Parental authority comes in two forms: negative and positive. You may establish negative authority by ruling with fear. While this can bring some degree of apparent obedience, it simultaneously fosters underlying resentment that urges the child toward destructive retaliation and rebellion. At the same time, it causes the child to feel pointlessly unhappy, ineffectual, out of control, and worthless.

You experience a positive sense of authority in your relationship with your child when you elicit his happy, willing cooperation with no more than an occasional, minimal and fleeting show of resistance. Your child cooperates because he wants to—out of his genuine feelings of respect and appreciation for you, inspired by his trust in your judgment.

You Must Earn It

Parents unwittingly undermine their potential for positive authority when they expect to receive it based on entitlement. A child needs to trust the person in charge to genuinely respect the person in charge enough to *want* to cooperate. Children enter life trusting totally. Something *we* do changes that.

Your child will place you in a position of positive authority as you demonstrate alert responsiveness to his real needs and interests. Your positive authority happens naturally as you harmonize with the child at a deep enough level to inspire her trust and confidence in your leadership. This requires you to recognize and empathize with your child's deeper feelings. To the extent that you clash with your child you demonstrate a lack of accurate awareness of her inner life.

Respect Yourself

You teach your child to relate to you as you relate to yourself. Your child will show a lack of confidence in you to the extent that you lack confidence in yourself. If you drive yourself so hard that you feel over-taxed and over-burdened, or if you over-indulge and allow your own greater potential to languish, you demonstrate a lack of respect for yourself that will lead your child to treat you in disrespectful ways. Your child's attitude toward you will reflect and reinforce the attitude toward yourself that you harbor. As you adhere to your integrity, go for what you truly want in life, and treat yourself well, your child will demonstrate a basic level of deep respect in how she relates with you.

Be Big About It

Power of authority. Maintain your peace and poise, and cultivate an attitude that stays above all struggles. Instead of locking horns in conflict with your child, stop struggling, step back and strategize. You will find your opportunity to successfully assert leverage, but not if you quibble away your power in pointless, personal squabbles.

"Old School" Authority

In "the old days" adults believed they had to crush the child's will to produce a well-behaved adult. The child was treated as an inferior. Today we know that approach deeply damages the budding self-respect of the developing human being. It prepares one even in adulthood to accept unfair treatment, or it drives one to compensate by seeking unfair advantage of others.

At the opposite end of the spectrum we find the excessively liberal style of parenting in which the child rules the parents into blind submission. These parents teach their child to consider no one's feelings but his own. The parent weakly or meekly fails to establish boundaries that clearly define the child's responsibilities and teach mutual respect.

Positive parental authority demonstrates unconditional respect for *both* parent and child, and for the world-environment as a whole. We can call this "True School" authority and it has had its proponents for a very long time, including the likes of Maria Montessori and Rudolph Steiner, and, more recently, Dr. Alice Miller. One can trace its roots, even, to the heart of Judaism, Christianity and Buddhism.

The S.E.A.T. Of Authority

Your establishment of positive authority in your relationship with your child ultimately rests on your authority over yourself. You have to treat yourself well and make good choices in your responses to be effectively in charge in your relationship with your child. Authority over yourself manifests as you align your actions and reactions with your aims instead of being ruled by automatic, emotional reaction habits.

A simple formula, which I call *The S.E.A.T. of Authority*, can help you remember how to achieve this. The formula highlights four basic forces – your **S**peech, **E**motion, **A**ction and **T**hought – that you need to direct for authority.

"S" Is For Speech

Command authority by speaking with clarity, guided by purpose. In other words, express yourself in a way that makes you easily understood and wastes no energy on pointless prattle. Speak to the point, in a voice of calm, compassionate confidence. Eliminate pleading and complaining. Avoid sounding hopeless or helpless, overwhelmed or out of control. Apologize and admit mistakes when called for, but do so in a manner that expresses unconditional self-respect.

Don't confuse an arrogant speaking style with the air of true authority. Arrogance conveys an underlying belief in one's own inadequacy and elicits distrust and disrespect from the listener. Don't talk down to your child or you instigate his drive to oppose your will just to prove his power.

"E" Is For Emotion

To the extent that your child can "make" you react with negative emotion, you teach her to act like the one in charge. To be perceived and treated as a positive authority figure, maintain even-tempered control over your emotional reactions. Consistently express the attitude of confidence in yourself, in your child, and in the positive potential of all situations. Without this, you exude insecurity which your child will pick up, causing her to lack confidence in you. In general, to the extent that intense emotional reactions rule you, you appear out of control, unstable, and unreliable, which incites a child to struggle for control out of a sense of insecurity.

"A" Is For Action

You naturally command the respect and cooperation of one in a position of authority as you consistently take action in line with your deepest, truest values. Your style of action expresses your level of authority as well. Routinely exhibiting rush, frenzied chaos, and disorganized messiness portrays you as one *out* of control. Carry yourself with grace and dignity around your child. You need to *act* in charge in order to be perceived as in charge.

"T" Is For Thought

Devote some time every day to deep contemplation upon what really matters to you. You can then evaluate the direction you are headed in and make necessary adjustments. Real authority over oneself begins with authority over one's own thinking. Notice how much though you waste on worrying about how others think about you. Your choices need to be based on what you believe is best for your child regardless of others' opinions.

Think more about what you want than what you don't want (as your life literally *heads* in the direction that you think about). Think more about how to support what is working than about what you fear might undermine or stand in your way. Expect everything to work out and it will.

End Disrespect

To end your child's disrespectful way of relating with you, maintain your respectful way of relating with yourself *and* your child. Your consistent modeling of respect leads him into conduct that demonstrates respect for himself and others. When you react with much anger and stress, you treat yourself poorly, which expresses a lack of self-respect.

When you feel disrespected by your child, take a closer look at what is actually going on. You are interpreting your child's behavior in a way that makes you feel disrespected. In other words, *you make yourself experience disrespect.*

Feeling disrespected makes one feel powerless and defeated. It provokes angry lashing out and resorting to the use of intimidation to win. But this will never work with your child. You will experience more ease and satisfaction in guiding your child's behavior as you maintain your feeling of calm and confident respect for yourself and for your child no matter how your child behaves.

Chapter 6
The G.A.T.E. Of Self-Control

Self-control means that you can choose your response based on the results you want, instead of blindly reacting to what happens. How you respond to your child influences what your child does next. Four basic laws govern your ability to choose your responses. Function counter to these laws and you will find it virtually impossible to avoid angry, frustrating, counter-productive reactions to your child's behavior. Heed these laws and it becomes increasingly easy to maintain your wise and loving self-control during even the most challenging of times. I refer to these laws as *The G.A.T.E. Of Self-Control*. This formula highlights four basic forces—your **G**rowth, **A**wareness, **T**ime and **E**nergy.

"G" Stands For Growth By Small Degrees

With regular exercise, self-control **G**rows like the strength of a muscle. Practice handling every situation in a peaceful mode, particularly when you feel most tempted to lose your composure. Your power of improved self-control **G**rows only by small degrees. Be satisfied with even the tiniest degrees of increased calm in your way of dealing with what happens. Small degrees of change gradually build momentum, eventually leading to major breakthroughs. As your self-control **G**rows, you can choose responses that better align with the outcomes you really want.

"A" Stands For Awareness

You cannot maintain your self-control if you are not **A**ware of yourself while you are losing it. Avoid getting so distracted by other things, or so focused on your child's behavior, that you overlook the way you react. Pay attention to how *you* feel, act, speak and think to recognize when you begin entering anger or stress. The sooner you become aware of yourself losing your peace and poise, the sooner and more easily you can pull yourself out of that reaction.

"T" Stands For Time

To preserve sane self-control, you must move through **T**ime in a patient, unrushed manner. Give yourself the time you need to function calmly and capably. Rush drives you out of self-control by pushing you to the edge of your patience, *forcing* you to overreact with anger and stress when your child's behaviors mismatch your expectations. The stress of rush drives you to clash with your child's healthy, natural pace, making him seem uncooperative when, in fact, your pushy, nervous war against time makes him seem so difficult. When you catch yourself rushing, reflect on what happened and think creatively about how you could have handled the situation without rush. Routinely clarify your priorities in order to avoid wasting time on non-essentials. Trust the best you can do without rush because that truly is the best you can do.

"E" Stands For Energy

You cannot routinely violate your **E**nergy limitations without serious consequences. A run down, worn out state makes you more susceptible to illness, let alone unbalanced and destructive emotional reactions. In fact, it takes an abundance of energy to maintain the self-control you need to function well. A low energy state turns the normal challenges of daily living into increasingly difficult and unpleasant burdens. When you feel tired or low in energy, it might seem like your child has a behavior problem when, actually, the problem you experience stems from your lack of the energy it takes to easily handle her behavior with calm competence.

Don't waste energy on trivial or negative thought, speech, or emotional reactions. Look for the most energy-efficient way of doing everything. Notice how different people, environments and activities impact your energy level. Stay away from those that drain you, or at least minimize your involvement with them. Eating too much or too little, getting too little rest or too little physical exercise *guarantees* that you lack the energy you need to preserve your self-control amid the pressures of daily living. TV viewing has a negative impact on energy as well; the more you watch, the more negative you feel.

And, by the way, nothing burns energy *more quickly* than functioning at a rushed or hectic pace, or reacting with intense negative emotion. The best solution to a low energy state is simply to stop pushing and give yourself some rest. Don't regard this as a luxury, but as an absolute necessity for effective, healthy, happy parenting.

PART TWO

INFLUENCES THAT SHAPE YOUR CHILD'S BEHAVIOR

Chapter 7
The Law Of Reflection

Your child's behavior, mood, attitude and values reflect back the behavior, mood, attitude and values expressed in her environment. I call this *The Law of Reflection.* In this chapter, we will explore how you can use this law to guide your child's behavior.

Control The Influences

The child exposed to angry, hyper, insecure adults feels angry, hyper and insecure. The child exposed to a bully learns to bully. The child who repeatedly has his toy stripped from him by another, learns to snatch things from others. This is The Law Of Reflection in action. By taking control of the surrounding influences impacting the formation of your child's behavior, you take control of some of the major factors shaping your child's behavior and personality development.

The Foundation Plane

We err when we presume that if a child is too young to comprehend what goes on around him, what goes on around him has no impact. During the first six years of life, the bedrock of your child's character and personality traits take shape to form the foundation plane of his development. In other words, altering this time lodge the deepest and strongest to form patterns that may last a lifetime. If your child is older than six, obviously, it is not too late to guide her behavior and to influence the formation of her character, but you will never again have the immensity of the power of influence that you possess in the first six years.

You Radiate All You Are

To make the most of The Law Of Reflection, think of your child at every age as absorbing *everything* you say, think, feel and do and bound to reflect that back in some fashion. The child exposed to parents who speak disrespectfully to one another will soon demonstrate a similar show of disrespectful self-expression. When you exude much impatience around your child, you literally teach your child to be impatient. Trying to improve your child's behavior without first improving your own is as futile as expecting your reflection in the mirror to change without first changing your physical appearance. Your child will demonstrate a higher level of positive self-control as you raise your own level of positive self-expression.

Seed-Soil-Fruit

Imagine trying to grow a tomato plant with apple seeds! Trying to "make" a child demonstrate more flexible and considerate cooperation by routinely clashing with his will and reacting in ways that hurt his feelings and make him feel stifled makes no more sense.

I sometimes refer to The Law Of Reflection as The Law Of Seed-Soil-Fruit, based on the premise that the way that you behave around your child or toward your child enters your child like a seed planted in the fertile soil of her personality. Each time you repeat that behavior in your child's vicinity you nurture that seed until it eventually blooms into the fruit of a similar behavior coming from your child. The Law Of Reflection reinforces the principle that you reap what you sow in relation to your child.

Self-Work

Do you yell? Do you argue? Do you blame others instead of taking responsibility for your contribution to your problems? Do you lose your temper and lash out harshly in reaction to a person's mistake? Are you in too much of a hurry? Are you too passive and indirect, too defensive, too unfocused, or too intense and aggressive in your manner of speaking? Do you drive yourself so hard that you feel irritated, unhappy and ungrateful? See all of this as ways that you lead your child into behaving similarly.

Closely and honestly observing how you act and react is the first step to making positive use of The Law Of Reflection. The next step is to apply the self-discipline needed to gradually eliminate from your own self-conduct ways of functioning that you do not want your child to replicate, and to practice ways of living, relating, and dealing with things that you want to see your child exhibiting. Working on your own conduct not only improves your child's conduct; it teaches your child to take responsibility for his own behavior and to work on improving his self-conduct.

A Shift Toward Humility

As you attempt to improve your influence upon your child in this way, you will find that you do not behave as perfectly as you may have assumed, that improving one's behavior or attitude proves more difficult than you imagined, and that your child's worst behavior is no worse than your own and probably less harmful. With this more humble perspective, you can respond with more understanding and compassion when your child does not live up to your expectations. This more loving response will teach your child to be more kind, loving, and respectful toward others and toward herself.

Look Beyond Yourself

To use The Law Of Reflection fully, observe the behavior of *everyone* around your child. As consistently as possible, and with definite intention, provide your child with demonstrations of the behavior that you want and eliminate from his surroundings any behaviors, moods or attitudes that you do not want your child to display.

How To Lead

You can use The Law Of Reflection to lead your child into activity. Let your child see you doing it; then invite her to join you. You have observed that children want to do whatever they see done around them. As you do what you want your child to do, and do it in a way that makes the activity look enticing, you harness the power of The Law Of Reflection that drives your child to do as you do.

To have your child speak respectfully to you, don't harshly criticize or talk down to him when he sounds rude. Correct him by saying, "This is how I want you to say that..." and then say it exactly as you want to hear it, trusting that The Law Of Reflection impels your child to repeat what he has just observed.

Don't Fight Results

When you do not want your child to repeat an action or attitude exhibited around him, change his surroundings. In fact, the first place to look whenever you feel concerned about your child's self-conduct is to your child's environment. Until you eliminate the cause, you waste your time fighting against the result.

Teaching Self-Control

Based on The Law Of Reflection, you cannot improve your child's self-control while you are losing yours. To lead your child into more calm, responsible self-conduct, demonstrate that at a higher level yourself, *particularly when you do not care for your child's behavior.* How you react to your child's behavior teaches your child to react similarly when she does not get her way. Rather than justifying your loss of composure, focus on improving it. Otherwise, you merely teach your child to justify her own destructive reactions.

Society's Child

Basically, The Law Of Reflection expresses that children become whom they spend time with. We cannot reasonably expect children to behave well in the society of children or adults behaving poorly. Everything your child sees on TV, hears on the radio, encounters on the Internet or observes in her immediate environment goes in like a seed.

Expose your child to the finest modeling. Take an honest look at how adults and children conduct themselves around your child and gauge the extent to which they function consistently with your core values. Minimize your child's exposure to individuals who exhibit much anger, depression, insecurity, or lack of integrity, as well as to those who display rude, crude or chaotic behavior.

While it is true that you cannot control every influence in your child's environment, you can control a great deal, and that much is your responsibility. Regard the way others behave around and toward your child as a foreshadowing of your child's future behavior. Be ready and willing to "time-out" anyone, including a relative, whose attitude or conduct you do not wish your child to replicate.

Parenting With Integrity

You provide your child with the very best influences possible by becoming the very best person you can be. Based on The Law Of Reflection, you cannot teach a child right from wrong. You teach a child right only from right. When your child displays less than honorable conduct, take a deeper, more honest look at your own forms of moral weakness and set to work on self-improvement.

When it comes to leading children into ethical conduct, our actions speak so loudly that they drown out what we say. You cannot hide from children what you are. Your innermost feelings and attitudes radiate and children absorb it. The attempt to hide our improper or destructive conduct merely teaches them to hide their own, not to face it and strive to repair it.

To the extent that you depart from the path of your own integrity, you lack respect for yourself. This teaches your child to behave in ways that cost his self-respect. The child who does not respect himself does not care enough about himself to make choices in his own best interest and is therefore more easily led down self-destructive paths.

Discipline With Discipline

The Law Of Reflection makes clear that one should never discipline a child using a behavior one does not wish the child to repeat. Yelling, nagging, bickering, issuing verbal put-downs, withdrawing love, or spanking in any form teaches the child to behave in exactly those ways. In Part 4 we will look at your specific response-options for child discipline. But to be constructive, they cannot conflict with The Law Of Reflection. For now, begin improving your child's behavior by taking a closer look at your own, and then make a deeper commitment to living true to your higher values.

Past Mistakes

There are no perfect parents. Once you learn about The Law Of Reflection you are bound to see mistakes you have made. Face these for the lessons they provide as to how to do better from now on and focus on making the most of your present opportunities to provide your child with the best possible modeling influences from now on.

Chapter 8
Your Child's S.T.E.M. Universe

Since children tend to replicate what we expose them to, you pit yourself against an irresistible power when you attempt to change a behavior without changing the environmental conditions that the behavior reflects. As has been stated, to improve a behavior, the first place to look is to your child's surroundings because your child's behaviors, moods and attitudes reflect the conditions of their environment.

While even adults are impacted by what goes on around them, the younger the child, the more deeply impacted is the child by the condition of their surroundings.

Raised By Dogs

The Law Of Reflection extends beyond direct human influence. My son's immediate surroundings during his first couple of years of life included our three, large, active dogs who often had their tongues hanging out. Can you guess where Gabriel's tongue spent much of the time? What if I attempted to teach him to keep his tongue in his mouth through harsh discipline, while continuing his exposure to those dogs? This would be like trying to get a child to stop speaking Italian by yelling at him in Italian. I would have been reinforcing the very behavior I am struggling to change and making him feel very unhappy, confused and inadequate in the process.

A child exposed to an aggressive pet will demonstrate aggressive tendencies, just as the child exposed to an adult who treats a pet aggressively will do the same.

Beyond Living Creatures

The conditions of inanimate objects also influence a child via The Law Of Reflection. By providing your child with physical surroundings that express order and beauty, intelligence, sensitivity, and attention to detail, you influence the formation of your child's behavior and personality in a way that makes her more capable of demonstrating those qualities herself.

Your Child's S.T.E.M. Universe

Your child's environmental influences can be categorized into four basic elements referred to by my mentor, Isidore Friedman, in *Organic Education*, as the child's "S.T.E.M. Universe." These include:

S: The **S**patial qualities of your child's surroundings
T: The **T**iming of your child's environments
E: The **E**nergy influence of your child's environment
M: The qualities of the **M**aterial objects around your child

Take Charge Of Your Child's Spatial Universe

Cramped, cluttered, disorganized surroundings incite frustration and contribute to temperamental meltdowns. Messiness and the presence of too much stuff induce lethargy, melancholy and disinterest. Dirty environments teach slovenliness. Disarray prompts disorderly behavior and chaotic emotional reactivity.

Provide your child with neatly arranged and ordered spaces that permit a smooth flowing motion through the environment. Straighten the pictures on the wall, even the blinds on the windows, and arrange things generally in an orderly fashion. Orderly conditions help the child to act and to think in an orderly manner and to experience and express harmonious feelings. *However, do not enforce perfection of order, cleanliness or neatness to the point that the child cannot relax and behave naturally, or feels that you care more about the quality of the environment than about her.*

Provide your child under six years of age with one corner of every room in your home that contains his personal things, an area that he feels is his own. Give children under six a personal mat they can play on, which defines their personal space and helps them to feel safely contained and responsible within their personal boundaries. Place the things your small child needs within his reach so that he develops more independence and self-reliance. Place out of his reach and sight objects you do not want him to have or to demand.

Take Charge Of Your Child's Time Universe

When you place a child in a particular environment matters. When she feels tired, for instance, she needs more peace and quiet and familiarity in her surroundings. When she first wakes in the morning or goes to bed at night, she wants to see familiar faces and familiar objects.

Monitor the pace of change in your child's environment as well. If things change too rapidly, too unpredictably or too abruptly the child feels disturbed and is more prone to act out in a disturbing fashion.

Do your best to provide children, particularly those under six, with as much predictability of surroundings as possible. Produce a regular routine of environments for them so they find themselves in the same environments at the same time and for the same amount of time on a routine basis. For instance, you will find your child napping better if naptime always happens at a particular time, in a particular location. She will handle leaving the playground more easily if she goes to the playground the same day, the same time, and for the same amount of time on a routine basis. If your child seems unsettled, chaotic, unpredictable, take a look at your child's environmental schedule to see if you have too much unpredictability there.

Take Charge Of Your Child's Energy Universe

Provide your child with surroundings that energize and uplift, soothe and comfort her. Dirty, messy settings depress children, as they do adults. Poor lighting and stifling, stagnant air lower a child's vitality and motivation.

Fill her living space with bright – not glaring - light during the day (to promote good cheer) and soft, mellow lighting when you want her to settle down. Open the windows (even in winter, for short times) to let fresh air in (to help her feel physically, emotionally and mentally refreshed and clear).

Clean the windows to permit clear views of the outside world. This helps your child feel more free, open and involved with life. Clean windows also permit a higher quality of sunlight that promotes a brighter mind and lighter mood.

Place living samples of nature in his surroundings, like plants and flowers, which share with him their life force, as well as their tenderness, their beauty and charm.

Be particularly aware of the energy levels of the *people* around your child. Distressed, morose, disgruntled, frustrated people exude their negativity like a gravitational pull, dragging down the spirit of the child. Happy, healthy, caring people functioning in a calm, orderly manner and relating with one another harmoniously nurture and elevate your child with positive energy.

Take Charge Of Your Child's Material Universe

Your child's behavior, mood and attitude will reflect, to some extent, the appearance and condition of the material objects surrounding her. Repair broken objects (broken things promote disrespect for objects and bodies). Introduce pleasant and interesting objects (like a picture of a stream in the woods), sounds (like the sound of trickling water or soft music), smells (mild, natural pleasant fragrances), textures (like velvet, silk, and smoothly hewn objects made of fine natural materials). Connect your child to the higher levels of beauty and genius by placing things such as replicas of masterpieces in her surroundings. Play Mozart. Read Shakespeare aloud (even if you don't understand the words yourself).

Give your child geometric forms to handle and to see. The perfect symmetry of these objects molds orderly behavior, tranquil feelings and sharp thinking.

Be sure to have objects in your child's environment suited to his size, like chairs that he can easily place himself on or off, eating utensils that he can easily handle, a broom like the one you use but sized to be manageable for him. Hang pictures on the wall at her eye level. All of this provides a child with a sense of belonging and prepares her for self-reliance.

Routinely Survey Your Child's S.T.E.M. Universe

Routinely examine your child's surroundings and evaluate their influence upon her. It does not require more money to create more supportive S.T.E.M. environments. It takes creativity and determination, and a willingness to make small changes if that is the best you can do at the time. Even a miniscule improvement like tidying up one small area of mess or clutter or making a small improvement to the lighting helps a child to think, feel and act at a higher level. Hyperactive children especially need to have their exposure to intense, chaotic surroundings minimized as much as possible.

The Universe Outside

A common mistake parents make is to presume that the child needs negativity at home to be able to handle the negativity in the world outside of home. The opposite proves true. The better your child's home conditions support your behavior and attitude goals for your child, the less influenced he will be by the negative, chaotic conditions of the world outside. Harmonious home life makes one stronger and more capable of handling the influences outside of home.

Chapter 9
The Art Of
Pleasing And Displeasing Your Child

While on a long car trip, eight-year-old Ellen asked her mother to stop at a particular fast-food restaurant for lunch. Her mother explained that that restaurant was not located at this exit, and there was no telling how long they would have to drive before they reached one. Ellen plunged into one of her typical sulking routines.

Although her mother felt tempted to coax her daughter out of her pout, she decided to *not* make that her job and focused on maintaining her own pleasant peace and poise instead. To her surprise and delight, Ellen quickly stopped sulking and brightened up. Her mother felt amazed at how easily things worked out. It even seemed to her that Ellen began showing her more respect because the sulking did not succeed at manipulating her.

The Strength To Displease

Fostering your child's responsible behavior sometimes requires you to call upon the inner strength to endure your child's displeasure. Your wise parental judgment, not your weak emotional reaction, needs to guide your decisions. If your child's display of discontent overly controls you, she learns to use unhappiness to get what she wants, which can ultimately lead her into depression. You also rob her of the opportunity to develop the inner strength to constructively handle difficulty and disappointment. Making hasty efforts to rescue a child from feelings of displeasure makes him more dependent and more helpless, less self-reliant and less helpful.

Balancing Act

The art of *responsibly* pleasing and displeasing your child is a true balancing act. You have to consider the consequences of pleasing or displeasing *before* doing either. Being too harsh and inflexible causes a child too much frustration, driving him into angry rebelliousness and sinking him into a depressing feeling of isolation and abandonment. Being overly passive, permissive, indulgent, or helpful confuses the child about her responsibilities.

As a general rule, when you must refuse your child what he wants, be compassionate in your feelings toward him. Do not wall yourself off from him emotionally. Immediately resume your loving way of relating. If he closes off or pushes you away, be patient; but also be ready to make the first move at the first sign of an opening for loving reconnection.

Teach Your Child Boundaries

Teaching a child appropriate boundaries is not the same as teaching the child that he is too limited in his abilities or worth to even deserve what he wants. It is about teaching your child *how* to get all he wants out of life through responsible, respectful and compassionate self-conduct.

Numerous times during the day, nine-year-old Alec spoke rudely to his mother and to other adults. He brutishly shoved a child out of his way in the library. He ignored his mother when she told him to stop doing cartwheels so close to his baby sister at the top of the stairs and then, when she pointed out that his shoes had come untied, he demanded that she tie his shoelaces for him and without hesitation she stooped over and did his bidding. At the end of the day he played his video game while waiting for his mother to prepare and serve dinner.

Although his mother occasionally complained about his behavior at various times during the day, she took no real action to make his appropriate boundaries clear. You really cannot blame a child for overstepping boundaries when no one has taught him where exactly they are.

Where To Draw The Line

When asked why she did not take away his video game as a consequence for his antics during the day, Alec's mom gave two reasons. First, she said that she knew how much he liked playing his video game and she liked to see him happy. Second, she said that if she imposed that consequence, she fully expected that Alec would throw a tantrum that *she* found unpleasant. Because she lacked the inner strength to endure Alec's displeasure, she taught him to please himself without regard for his impact upon others.

How Much Is Too Much

Never confuse the following with *constructively* displeasing a child:

- Directing harsh, angry criticism at the child
- Displaying much annoyance, disappointment or impatience with the child
- Nagging, yelling, hotly arguing with or hitting a child
- Coldly withdrawing your loving involvement from the child
- Making the child feel unsafe, either emotionally or physically

Such overly severe reactions obfuscate a child's sense of appropriate boundaries at least as much as do excessively indulgent responses. At the same time, they wound a child's self-esteem and self-confidence, making him prone to more destructive behavior.

While you must sometimes allow your child to feel badly, and sometimes make decisions that will cause him to feel unhappy, never do anything with the aim of making him feel badly, for that constitutes cruelty and teaches the child to mistreat himself and others.

Be Honest With Yourself

Sometimes a child's unhappiness expresses a legitimate need that we must address. Sometimes what the child needs is for her parent to allow her to feel dissatisfied and displeased. To determine which response your child needs from you, you need to be honest with yourself as you ask yourself:

- "Why am I giving in to—or denying—this demand or request?"
- "What am I really accomplishing by helping him—or hurting him—in this way?"

Look Back And Learn

After you please your child or rescue her from discontent, review the situation and consider if your child would have been better served by you allowing her to experience more difficulty. If you withhold your support and let her experience unhappiness, review the situation to consider if a more lenient, helpful response would have served her better. Do this review not to instill self-doubt, but to deepen and clarify your understanding for more effective decision-making in the future.

Examine Your Motives

If you react in haste or from emotion or habit, you are bound to misjudge and end up negatively impacting your child. You have to take a look at what motivates *you* before giving your child what she asks for or demands, or refusing to do so.

Are you giving in out of weakness based on fear of your child's displeasure, fear of him not liking you or fear of his tantrum? Are you over-indulging her to impress others with how much you can give?

Are you displeasing your child because you demand too much control? Are you being mean? Are *you* just being difficult?

Concentrate on your intention to do that which truly serves your child's best interest, in support of his development into a fine, strong, able and loving human being. Hold that intention in mind—hold it in your heart—and it will guide you like an internal compass.

Chapter 10
The Child Development Formula

Take a look at my formula representing child behavior and development:

$$(? P) - (C) = (SI) = (B)$$

The symbols stand for:

(?) Infinite (P) Potential
(–) Minus (C) Criticism
(=) Equals (SI) Self-Image
(=) Equals (B) Behavior

? P (Infinite Potential)

The "? P" represents your child's—every child's—infinite potential. All children, including those we label "disabled", possess a pathway to infinite development, a gift, a facet of personality or being that extends into the realm of the miraculous.

No one can define the real limits of any human being's potential, not with any true basis in fact. You can imagine limits. You can presume limits. But no one really knows for certain what is possible for anyone. What we do know, however, is that if you expect less of someone, you increase the likelihood of getting less.

When it comes to raising children, as in every other area of life, we see what we look for. Keep your child's infinite potential in mind and think of it as her true self or essential nature. This will help you keep her limitations and her missteps in perspective, so you can avoid over-reacting to what you do not want. To bring out a child's positive potential, focus mostly on what the child does right or well, and direct most of your efforts into supporting that.

Your child has infinite potential and so do you!

– C (Minus Criticism)

The "- C" signifies that you take away from your child's ability to fulfill his potential when you play the role of detractor. In other words, by imposing a negative view or opinion onto your child, you subtract some of his capacity to demonstrate the greatness within him.

Calling your child weak, helpless, selfish, stubborn, incapable, irresponsible or trouble blinds you *and blinds your child* to the limitless possibilities of who she truly is and all that she can become, which, in turn, prevents you from seeing – and from doing – all you can to support her fulfillment of greater potential.

You express criticism not just through your spoken words, but also through your silent attitudes and actions. Treating a child with less than total respect, doing too much to help, rejecting a child and withdrawing your love, even worrying about your child turning out to be a disappointment, all reaches your child and influences him negatively.

= SI (Equals Self-Image)

Think of yourself as a sort of mirror reflection that teaches your child who she is. The child repeatedly exposed to a negative, demeaning, critical view of himself accepts that as a true reflection of his identity. For example, the more you relate to your child as weak, helpless, difficult or dependent, the more he identifies with that negative characterization and believes it to be who he is.

= B (Equals Behavior)

How a person sees herself, her self-image or self-concept, plays a crucial role in how she behaves. *In fact, children, as well as adults, behave in line with their self-image.* The child who receives the message, "You are a selfish brat," will see herself as a brat and then prove those negative views to be correct through her self-conduct. While all human beings display some selfishness, focusing too much attention on that weakness and making too big of a deal about it influences a person to demonstrate that quality more, not less.

Your child's self-image translates into the behavior he demonstrates. A person who sees himself as incapable or as undeserving cannot make a full effort to achieve at a higher level. In the past we believed we could help a child behave more appropriately and perform at a higher level by fiercely criticizing his mistakes and shortcomings. However, now we know that children who receive too much harsh criticism exhibit lower levels of competence.

The Period Of No-Defense

In the first six years of life, a child has virtually no defense against the identity-shaping influences coming from outside of her. As she matures beyond the sixth year, she has a growing capacity to practice discrimination as to what she will and will not accept about herself. However, even with older children and adults, over-exposure to a negatively critical view of oneself has a way of getting in and being believed.

Protect Your Child's Self-Image

Think of your words as building blocks of your child's self-image. By labeling your child "rude," "bossy," "wild," "obnoxious," "lazy, " "selfish," "stupid," or "bad," your words create that image of herself in her mind. Her subsequent behavior then follows the pattern of that image.

Protect your child, as much as possible, from the destructive critical messages sent her way from others. If he receives negative messages about himself from adults other than you, or even from siblings, friends or classmates, it has the same negative influence upon his self-image and behavior.

How To Use This Formula

To use this formula as a sort of map showing you the way to help your child fulfill his glorious potential, regard your child's behavior as an expression of his self-image. For example, if he consistently lets his homework slide, regard that as a probable indication that he views himself as a weak or incapable student. To raise his level of performance, he first has to see himself as someone capable of higher performance. Help him to improve his self-image by focusing his attention on what he does well. Show genuine appreciation for his gifts and talents, and point out the ways he functions that you admire. Consistently relate to him in a way that demonstrates that you deeply value and believe in him and he will begin drawing upon his own greater power to succeed.

Closely observe your attitude toward your child. You may presume that you relate to her in a way that expresses your belief in her while actually relating to her as inadequate and inferior. Harping on her mistakes, showing much frustration or disappointment when her behavior displeases you, complaining about her performance or lack of progress and failing to recognize the greatness she already exhibits teaches her to see herself as a failure, and that self-perception programs her to fail.

Respond to your child's mistakes and missteps with compassion and with confidence. You have to believe in your child *before* she can demonstrate the level of performance you hope for. This means that you demonstrate unshakeable confidence, not insecurity or anxious worry about the direction she is headed in.

Relate with your child as if you really know that he is a great achiever, a blessing in your life, a totally good, kind, capable, brilliant, gifted—essentially limitless human being. This takes practice for some of us, for we have fallen into the habit of counting on our child's performance to encourage us, when what we need is to feel encouraged first.

Chapter 11
The Influence Of Vision And Expectation

One of the most potent parenting powers of influence that you possess, your ability to determine what mental image of your child you hold, may be one that you misuse the most. Sadly, many parents *think* that how they think of their child depends upon their child. The fact is, however, that how you think represents a choice that you make. By purposefully choosing positive thoughts about your child, you harness a great creative power of influence.

Creative Visualization

Superior performers in every field have long known about the power of creative visualization. Visualizing what you want to set into motion creates forces that help you to bring it about. Each time you feed a vision by refocusing your attention upon it, you direct more creative energy into the process of its manifestation.

Unfortunately, not only positive visions materialize; so do negative ones. If you have tried visualizing an outcome you want but found it not to work, take a closer look at what you think about. Most likely you also entertain ideas or mental visions of what you don't want. To make the most of your creative power of visualization, visualize what you want and eliminate or avoid mentally visualizing what you do not want. Every time you think about your child disappointing you, you break this rule.

Visualize Your Child

Your mental vision of your child acts somewhat as a self-fulfilling prophecy. Choose to dwell on thoughts about your child that you wish to come true. Abandon ideas about your child that cause you to feel worry, resentment, disappointment or frustration.

How you think of yourself also matters. If you think of yourself as a failure because your child does not do as you say, that image lowers your parenting abilities. As you read in the previous chapter, adults, like children, live up to *or down to* the image of themselves that they hold in their minds.

The Organic Process

Intentional visions arise in an organic way, like flowers that bloom in your garden. The seed is your intention to envision a positive scene in your mind. Nurture that seed through slight, unstrained effort to imagine what you want to see. Just as you give a seed time to absorb water before giving it more, give your subconscious time to absorb and respond to your intention. After attempting to envision what you want, relax your effort; then, try again. Then, relax again. Repeat this until gradually, over time, your positive vision blooms vividly in your mind.

Cleanse Your Mind

If you and your child have been clashing for a while, seeing the two of you in harmony may not even be possible right now. However, nothing can improve until you improve the way you see things. Just as you weed a garden to protect the flowers and plants, you need to "weed" your mind of negative images whenever they occur. Negative images choke the life out of positive possibilities.

Begin cleansing your mind of negative images by closely observing your thinking throughout the day. When you see yourself engaging in a negative vision, quickly let that vision go. Think about what you want to happen instead or just focus on your present experience without thinking. If the negative image returns, reject it again. Do this over and over until negativity loses the power to control your mind.

Visioning With The Law Of Three

The more you keep your mind free of negative imagining, the more you can engage positive visualizations. Your ability to direct your imagination gains strength like the development of any muscle: through regular exercise. Spend at least a few minutes every single day intentionally envisioning what you want.

Following is a creative visualization exercise that incorporates The Law Of Three, addressed earlier.

* Envision yourself parenting calmly, confidently and competently with love. (Do this for 15 seconds.)
* Envision your child healthy, happy, loving, strong and behaving beautifully. (Do this for 15 seconds.)
* Envision the two of you relating as closely as a parent and a child can relate, in peace, harmony, mutual respect, joy and love. (Do this for 15 seconds.)

While lying in bed, sinking into sleep, try to focus on positive visions of yourself, your child and the relationship between you. As you drift off to sleep, mental visions sink most deeply into the subconscious mind and thus direct more creative energy into the manifestation of what you envision.

Visualize Specific Changes

Here is another exercise:

* Make a list of any specific behaviors that your child engages in that you would like to change. For instance, "My child sticks out his tongue more than I want him to."
* Describe the change you would like to see. For instance, "He keeps his tongue in his mouth when socially proper to do so."
* Then spend a few moments visualizing your child engaged in that new or higher level of behavior.

Another visualization exercise entails listing specific behaviors that you would like to see your child demonstrate. For instance, your list might include him dressing himself without your assistance each morning, putting his toys away before moving on to another activity and brushing his teeth willingly before going to bed. Then, go down that list and spend a few moments envisioning your child demonstrating each behavior.

Yet another exercise focuses on helping you to fulfill your higher parenting potential. Make a list of what your regard to be your parenting weaknesses. This list might include you raising your voice too much or arguing with your mate in front of the child. Perhaps you lose your patience with your child and express your frustration in a hurtful way. Include on this list any behavior that you engage in that has a negative influence upon your child. Then, go down that list and envision yourself doing the opposite. For instance, see yourself restraining yourself and choosing *not* to argue with your spouse in front of your child.

Teach Your Child Positive Visioning

You can begin teaching children as young as three-years of age to employ the power of positive visioning. Have your child close her eyes and then in a soft and soothing tone of voice, guide her to mentally picture herself healthy, strong and happy, with wonderful friends, getting along great with her parents, doing splendidly at school, helping out at home, feeling good about herself and growing up to fulfill a meaningful purpose in life.

When your child older than six struggles in any area of life, help him to envision the outcomes he wants, and teach him how to stop imagining what he does not want. Every evening at bedtime, engage in positive visioning together. If he has been struggling in school, see him easily getting great grades and understanding his work. If he has been struggling socially, envision him feeling confident in social situations. If he wants to lose weight of to get fit, envision him eating well and working out.

Also have him intentionally bring up a negative image he often dwells upon and then have him reject that image and replace it with an image of what he would like to happen instead. If he resists such exercises, saying that the positive images do not represent reality, explain that thought is a creative power that the most successful individuals learn how to harness and direct, to create what they want.

What Do You Expect?

Connected with the power of vision is the power of expectation. The steady, daily discipline of *dropping* negative expectations will relieve you of much destructive stress and empower you to fulfill your highest hopes. If you expect failure, you cannot totally try. As long as you expect success, you continue to go for it.

Ultimately, you *will* get what you expect. However, in between your expectation and your desired results, you often need to pass through disappointment. If you hold on to your positive expectation through these "valleys," your mental mastery grows and you send the strongest creative energy into the manifestation of what you expect.

Expect A Miracle

Jane, a single mother of two, was about to enter her front door after a long workday. She *expected* to enter "a pig sty and a zoo" *as usual.* She expected to feel humiliated, defeated and depressed as she futilely struggled to gain control *as usual.* In other words, she expected a repeat of the same old scene of parenting hell that she had experienced time and again.

Jane began practicing positive visioning and positive expectation on her way home from work every day. She tried seeing *and expecting* an orderly home in which her children behaved delightfully and treated her with love and respect. In the early stages of her practice, this was not easy. It seemed like it would take a miracle for things to improve. But over time, it became easier to expect that miracle as a real possibility.

She immediately found her stress diminishing and her positive attitude rising. This alone enabled her to exert a more positive, transformative influence on her children's behavior. When things did not match her expectation, instead of fighting and fretting, she preserved her confidence that her positive expectation would eventually come true.

Little by little she found herself feeling better on the way home and doing better upon her arrival. The steady improvement of her children's behavior followed.

PART THREE

THE CONSTRUCTION
OF YOUR CHILD'S PERSONALITY

Chapter 12
Planes Of Development

The child is not "done" upon emerging from the womb. No human being is ever really "done." The process of "self-creation" goes on throughout life. Every choice you make makes you, to some extent. From the beginning of your child's life, every experience she goes through and all that she does contributes to the formation of the behaviors and personality traits that she displays, both now and in the future.

One of our main tasks as parents consists in guiding the child's self-creation process to help the child to grow into a capable, responsible adult. Our principal ally in this work is the child herself, for her deepest drives and instincts impel her toward total mastery over her own destiny. We need to be careful not to squelch those drives through too much opposition to the child's will. At the same time, we are called upon to provide some direction to the child's environments and activities so these align with her best preparation for life in the world.

Planes Of Development

Most of us think of child development in terms of stages, but this can be misleading. Children do not actually *pass* from one stage to the next; they *build* one plane, tier or level of personality upon another, with the first plane of development serving as the foundation for all of the others. Your child's personality constructs on four succeeding planes as follows (read from the bottom up):

Plane Four: Eighteen through twenty-four
Plane Three: Twelve through eighteen
Plane Two: Six through twelve
Plane One: Birth through six

Plane One Work

During each plane of development, important developmental tasks present themselves. One primary task during the first six years of life, for instance, involves the child's development of the power of control over his own attention, including his ability to concentrate on a task and see it through to its completion. This fits into the larger task of developing work habits and fundamental skills that will support his further development and accomplishments all life long. You assist the child in fulfilling this task by challenging him to do as much as possible on his own.

During this period, Jake's father lacked the patience and self-control to let Jake fulfill his developmental tasks. As an example, when four-year old Jake started to build his train set, his father presumed that all Jake really cared about was playing with the completed set, so he took on the project himself, leaving Jake with little else to do but space out and clown around while he waited for his dad to complete the work for him. Jake's mother unwittingly impeded Jake's development by doing too much for him out of her desire to avoid dealing with a mess. For instance, she would not permit four-year-old Jake to pour liquid for himself from a container into a cup. Over time, because of his lack of practical engagement, Jake demonstrated a lack of confidence, motivation, and competence because he did not sufficiently exercise his capacities. Tragically, observing this prompted his parents to do even more for him and to expect less from him.

Plane Two Work

During the second six years, the child's horizons expand beyond the immediate family as he seeks to fit in with a group of friends with whom he feels comfortable and confident. Based on his previous experiences, Jake entered this phase of life with a weak attention and a lack of discipline causing him to become easily distracted and quickly bored. His schoolwork felt "too hard" for him to do and, once again, his parents bailed him out by doing too much of it for him. This only deepened his identification with the weak traits of helplessness and dependencies. As this plane begins identification with groups outside of the family, Jake rejected the more serious, studious children and gravitated toward the more playful and less responsible "characters."

Plane Three Work

Jake entered his third plane of development with the self-image of a poor student who hated school, avoided work as much as possible, and loved to hang out with others of that ilk. A primary drive during this plane of development is to stand out in the crowd. Jake sought the center of attention through reckless, daredevil antics that made him known for being outrageous and wild. His level of academic achievement remained low, and he got into more and more trouble, but by now his parents had long ingrained the pattern of expecting nothing better and continued coddling and rescuing him.

Plane Four Work

In the fourth and final plane of child development, occurring from age eighteen through twenty-four, the fledgling adult awakens to his sense of a life mission and the destiny he wishes to fulfill. During this stage Jake saw himself as intrinsically unconventional, discovered art and realized that he wanted to be an artist. But by now he lacked the discipline to focus and work even at what he loved, and so, despite himself, he continued to flounder.

By the time he reached the age of twenty-four, he felt such deep guilt and self-hate for lacking the discipline to make headway in his mission that he grew seriously depressed. His parents responded by giving him more "help," including financial support.

A Turning Point

You might be interested to know that Jake's story suddenly gets better; and how it gets better may give you insight into why it is never time to give up on a child.

At the nadir point of his depression, Jake met an artist much advanced in years who saw promise in Jake. Jake felt so inspired by this man's artistic mastery that he found the inner resolve to turn his life around and get on the track of his purpose and his passion. He had much to overcome, but he came to the realization that allowing his weak traits to rule would only bring him increasing misery.

Parenting Through The Planes

In the chapters that follow we will examine your child's primary developmental tasks in more detail and how you can take advantage of the special opportunity presented by each plane. I suggest that you read about every plane, not just the one your child presently occupies. By understanding your child's future planes you will gain insight into what you can do now to prepare your child to better deal with her upcoming challenges and opportunities. By understanding what your child needed in previous planes, you can better understand her present behavior and adjust your responses accordingly.

As your child matures, she gradually depends less on you for her continuing development. However, during each plane's construction there is much you can do to help your child take full advantage of her present developmental opportunities.

Chapter 13
Parenting Through The First Six Years

Your child's developmental urges press upon her from within like the force of life within a seed that drives it to sprout. Helping your child satisfy those urges contents her at the deepest level. This makes her feel loved, supported and understood, and it inspires her to relate sensitively and compassionately with others. Supporting a child's development does more than help the child to perform at a higher level in the future; it helps the child do that right now.

The Most Dependent Stage

The developmental urges of the child under six drive her into action, and the child depends upon the parent to channel that activity into safe and responsible development. For example, the infant places something in her mouth in order to learn the lessons of that sensory experience. The responsibility of the parent is to make sure that the object is clean and too large to choke the child.

The developmental drive of the child impels her to do what she sees done around her, as the first plane child almost entirely identifies with what goes on around her. The parent is responsible for surrounding the child with positive models.

Don't Work Too Hard

A parent's desire to help his child fulfill her glorious potential may cause the parent to try so hard to seize every possible developmental opportunity that he overly stresses himself and his child in the process. Causing a child too much stress not only hinders the developmental process, it promotes distressing child behavior and it can lead the child into ill health. By the same token, modeling any form of unbalanced behavior teaches the child to similarly (mis)function in an unbalanced manner.

The Absorbent Mind

The first plane child has what Maria Montessori termed, "the Absorbent Mind." This mind learns and develops through absorption of the influences of its surroundings, and the lessons and patterns it takes in can last for a lifetime. Your first plane child automatically adopts the modes of self-expression that you and others display around him.

To take advantage of this, routinely spend time with your child in situations that help you to experience sublime feelings like sacredness, wonder, holiness, awe, reverence, delight, love, forgiveness, deep inner peace, joy, and faith. While it helps a child at any stage to be exposed to such uplifting feelings, in the first six years it builds a sublime spiritual fortress at the core of your child's being that both protects and strengthens the sacred innocence of her pure heart and may serve as a sort of inner spiritual reservoir for the rest of her life.

The Child Is Like A Garden

Do your physical workouts in front of your first plane child. Let him see you reading and studying. Let her watch you working in an efficient manner, demonstrating excellence with joy. As she looks on, treat people, animals and objects with respect and care. To transmit the habits of hygiene, shave, brush your teeth and comb your hair while she watches. Every positive trait, behavior and attitude that you want for your child, "plant" in your child by demonstrating it around your child.

At the same time, practice being quite mindful of how you feel, act, speak and think around your child in order to recognize what you do *not* want your child to reflect. Discipline yourself to "weed out" and eliminate, or at least to diminish by whatever degree possible, those forms of self-expression that you do not want your child to adopt.

Developing Inner Fortitude

Taking him to the museum, the zoo, the aquarium, the beach is far preferable than dragging him to the mall where more superficial values are expressed. The more television he watches, the more commercialized and the less spiritualized his values become.

Turn your child's attention away from exhibitions of cruelty. If your first plane child witnesses much anger, fighting, unhappiness, brutality, selfishness or addictive patterns, she will accept these as her own at deep levels. Show him beauty and grandeur. Let him see you helping someone in need. Give him the experience of helping himself and others.

Don't expose her to frightening or disturbing scenes or experiences because you think that will make her stronger. Later in life, when she can place such scenes in perspective, she can handle them more constructively. In the first six years seriously disturbing experiences fracture the child's sense of security, causing her to resonate with an infant's feelings of horror, helplessness and overwhelm when reminiscent situations occur later in life.

Anchoring The Senses

During the first plane's development, anchor your child's physical senses to the physical world to help him to become alertly aware of his physical surroundings. Help your child awaken her eyes, ears, nose, taste and touch to the sensations of the physical universe. Point out physical details including the sensations of sight, sound, taste, touch and smell. This exercise balances her emotions, focuses her attention, and prepares her for practical life.

Constructive Activity

The constructive activity upon which your child concentrates acts upon your child as a construction process. Have him pile sticks gathered in the back yard, put toys in their appointed place, touch the keys on a piano in an ordered sequence or rhythmic fashion, carefully squeeze out a small dab of toothpaste onto his toothbrush, slip into your high heels and attempt to maintain her balance (where safe – for example, not at the top of the stairs), or mix honey into his hot cereal (with you close by to insure he does not burn himself). Challenging activities like these construct your child's skills and educate him about the way things work. Just because you find an act to be pointless from your perspective, to the first plane child it is all new, fascinating, fun *and developmental.*

Observe your child "at play" and you will see that she is actually going about serious work. (Though she does not know it herself, it is the work of self-creation.) Whatever she is doing, she is doing it with all of her might, focus and intention. As your child engages in work she becomes peaceful, happy, and develops greater self-discipline. Her ability to concentrate strengthens as she concentrates and she learns from every experience through which she passes. As the first plane child engages in safe activity that her own interest draws her into, she transforms into a new, more capable human being.

Avoid Power-Struggles

The child's lack of interest in an activity often indicates that she requires some other form of activity or engagement to achieve her next developmental stage. If she resists doing something, try changing your approach. If that does not work, see if you can help her find some other constructive activity to engage in. Avoid getting into *any* power-struggles or you instill in your child the pattern of habitually engaging in a power-struggle. When she grows frustrated in response to a difficulty she faces, offer just enough assistance for her to prevail using her full range of abilities.

When your child flatly resists doing something, step back and consider your options for responsibly relating with her without clashing with her will. The more you engage in a battle of wills with a first plane child, the more willful and less cooperative you make the child. So, unless absolutely necessary, seek ways of leading your child in which she wants to follow.

Twelve Essential "Ingredients"

Particularly during the construction of your child's first plane of development, the following twelve "ingredients," when provided in abundance, supply essential support for her immediate and long-term positive behavior and development:

- Loving feelings projected toward and around her
- Alert, non-critical attention paid to her
- Deep respect, appreciation, acceptance and approval showed to him
- Physical affection (that honors his safe and comfortable boundaries - for example, if he does not want to be held a certain way or by a certain person at a certain time, honor that)
- Freedom of activity (to actively exercise his physical abilities and explore his environment)
- Positive examples of responsible conduct
- Sensitive protection from physical harm or emotional distress
- Supervision through close physical involvement (instead of your futilely relying on verbal commands to direct)
- Pleasant quality time spent with you (to foster healthy bonding and deep feelings of self-worth)
- Peaceful, harmonious surroundings that evoke her feeling of security
- A stable, predictable, calm, unrushed daily routine
- Clear and consistently upheld boundaries correctly established (see Part Four) that teach her to set appropriate limits on her own behavior

How can you tell what, when and how much of *anything* your child needs? Through cautious trial and error and by careful observation of the child.

Twelve Harmful Influences

When you feel called upon to redirect or to correct your child's behavior, avoid doing so in a way that makes the child feel inadequate, wrong or worthless, as this just fuels his anger, insecurity and dependency, thus impeding his higher development. There are many things that the first plane child needs to receive *as little as possible*, including:

- Harsh criticism and angry blame
- Expressions of deep disappointment
- Exposure to anyone's temperamental outburst
- Exposure to any form of violence or cruelty
- Being overly controlled, opposed, restrained
- Being mocked, teased or receiving verbal put-downs
- Being forced to spend too much time away from those he loves the most
- Being rushed or continually prodded to move faster
- Having his focus of attention frequently interrupted
- Being made to feel a loss of self-confidence or self-worth
- Experiencing withdrawal of love or rejection from someone he loves
- Being made to feel intimidated, humiliated or powerless

The Time For Preschool

During the first three years of life, your child requires little more than his immediate family relationships and home environment for optimum development. From three to six she exhibits a readiness to spend three or four hours a day, five days a week, in a structured preschool setting (and structured camp setting in the summer).

The first plane child who spends too much time away from you receives too many influences beyond your control that impact him at the deepest level. During this period of rapid change, spending much time away from your child causes you to lose touch with who your child really is and how to best relate with her. The child during this stage of life who feels too separated from his parents and home may express his anger and insecurity through exceptionally fierce resistance to anyone's control.

Sensitivity To Order

Children under the age of six have a deep sensitivity to order and thus exhibit a strong need to order and arrange the objects and the people that surround them. By giving your child opportunities to create and to experience order *according to his sense of order*, he learns how to think, feel and act in an orderly manner and feels enough security to share control.

Because of her sensitivity to order, the child at this stage wants to get everything "right." This makes the years from two to six the ideal time for teaching your child the basic rules of grace and courtesy as well as appropriate and responsible behavior in general. The best way to help her to do things correctly is to help her to feel good about her best efforts, to demonstrate the right way, and to verbally inform her in a clear, consistent, compassionate way of the behavior that is not allowable when you need to redirect her.

Order Out Of Chaos

Occasionally permit your child to create a big mess. This gives him a healthy and satisfying sense of power over his world and the freedom of self-expression. It also allows him to see how a mess gets created. At the same time, it develops the physical coordination involved in creating the mess and provides some relief of built-up stress and tension.

When she is done creating her mess, pleasantly and politely engage her in cleaning up the mess. Don't approach this as a punishment, but as a fun task that you can do together. This exercise teaches her to bring order to chaos as it instills the lesson of cleaning up after oneself.

Think up creative ways to engage your child in creating order, bearing in mind that as she creates order she develops orderly behavior, harmonious emotions, and logical thinking abilities. You might lay out different size cups and place them in sequence from smallest to largest. Perform tasks carefully in front of your child as she watches you. Give her practice in activities that promote self-control like setting an object down on the table as quietly as possible. Present her with tiny objects to handle and manipulate *as you stand very close by and observe closely (to protect her from swallowing them)*. Involving your child in controlled action and in the use of fine motor skills brings over-all self-control and refinement to his thinking, feeling and action.

Mastery

The child in the first plane of development craves nothing more strongly than to experience mastery and accomplishment. Provide him with freedom and encouragement to test his abilities and attempt feats that he feels challenged by. Do not do more for her than necessary, but rather help her to do more and more on her own and for herself. With every accomplishment, the child develops competence and confidence that will help him to succeed at higher levels throughout his life.

Your first plane child will soon display a desire to try to do everything he sees being done. Though it slows you down, give him the opportunity to participate in your activities. Let him, for instance, hold the hammer you are using and show him how to use it. Welcome her "help" as you garden. Though this "help" might actually be a hindrance to your timely completion of the task at hand, he develops ability and skill through such involvement, as well as the habit of working and helping out. This also satisfies his need for bonding.

The first six years is the optimal time to develop your child's habit of contributing to household chores because he most strongly wants to do the chores he sees you doing and he feels a deep desire to experience the sense of contribution. Obtain for him a broom, a mop, a spray bottle suitable for his size and invite him to go to work with these items beside you and on his own.

Teach By Doing

You teach best during the first six years by demonstration, not by explanation. To teach your child how to do something, first ask, "May I show you how?" or "May I assist you?" When she gives you the okay, demonstrate the action slowly and silently as he watches. Then give him a try. His drive for mastery will keep him coming back to the action until he gets it right, or until he develops the level of skill and understanding he needs from it.

Successful Verbal Direction

The most common mistake made when attempting to direct children under six is to over-rely on words. The language of this stage is primarily non-verbal. They feel commanded from within to do what they see being done and to repeat what they themselves have done until they feel they have the act mastered.

To be as successful as possible with your words, describe what you *want* done, not what you do *not* want done. Your words create an image in the child's mind and first plane children feel instinctively driven to do what they see, whether they see it being done outside of them or in their minds. For instance, instead of saying, "Don't spill that," say something like, "Hold the cup steady and walk slowly and carefully to keep every drop within the cup."

Avoid Interrupting The Child's Focus

Allowing a first plane child to continue doing what he is doing until he feels done satisfies and cultivates the child's sense of order and it develops his ability to hold his focus of attention and to see things through. Routinely interrupting a child's focus weakens his attention, making him more easily distracted and more quickly bored. Additionally, if you routinely interrupt your child's focus of attention, you teach your child to interrupt and to disrupt others.

Therefore, avoid, or at least minimize, any interrupting of your child's concentration *when he is engaged in doing something safe and appropriate.* (TV viewing does not apply here, as that weakens a child's control over his attention and makes her more passive, unfocused and incompetent.) When your child seems to be ignoring you by staying focused on something else, don't take it personally. If you want your child's attention, quietly look at him until he looks up at you. He will do so momentarily. When he does so, that is the time to engage his attention. Protect your child from other children who continually attempt to distract his attention as well.

Repetition

Ever wonder why a toddler wants to watch the same DVD over and over and over, or to do the same basic activity countless times – until one day... no more interest? Repetition, like completion, satisfies and cultivates the child's sense of order and mastery. Her ability to predict what happens next provides her with a secure feeling of order and control that delights as well as comforts her. (She benefits most by experiencing repetition through activity far more than from passive TV viewing.) He will want to experience a particular form of repetition until he has drawn from it all the understanding and ability it has to offer him. When he can grow no more from it, he will want to leave it alone, and you would do well to honor that.

Surprise!

Contrary to what most of us seem to believe, children under six actually do not like surprises. They do much better when they know what to expect. Much irregularity in their routine unsettles them and makes it harder for them to settle down and function in an orderly manner.

A parent's surprising entrance into a child's environment when order has been established *without* that parent's presence often creates confusion in the child, to the point that it disrupts the child's emotional equanimity and sets off the child's disturbing behavior. This often happens when a parent arrives home from work when the stay-at-home parent has been with the child all day.

When you arrive in your child's environment, pay close attention to how your child responds. Certainly express your love and your pleasure, but contain yourself enough to sense her present state. She may need some time to make the adjustment and may seem a bit disconnected from you. In some cases, you may need to allow the person who has been in charge to remain in charge until you are alone with your child once again.

The Challenge Of Change

Transitions or changes of any kind cause every child's behavior to regress somewhat, and first plane children most of all. This includes periods when your child feels the stress of his own illness. Any change at all may prompt a child to become more withdrawn, more emotional, or more chaotic and aggressive. Moving a piece of furniture in a child's bedroom can cause her a sleepless night. The arrival of a new sibling can cause a regression in potty training. The presence of a new pet can drive him back to his pacifier. Any disruption in routine may produce a disruption in the child's behavior.

If you understand and expect the probability of this, it will be easier for you to handle. When you suspect that some form of change or transition lies at the root of a behavior problem, you can restore order more quickly and easily by:

- Making changes as gently and gradually as possible
- Remaining calm, kind and patient as she slowly recoups
- Re-introducing a stable order to the situation as soon as possible

Encourage Self-Reliance

From around the age of two, begin gently weaning your child off of counting on you to tote him around. Encourage him to walk on his own two feet, even when that slows you down. This reinforces his developing self-sufficiency. Encourage and allow as much self-reliance as he is capable of.

The child of three has the power to dress herself, make her bed, prepare her breakfast, and more. She can even adequately show other children how to do the things that she does. Giving your child responsibility makes her happier, more competent, and more confident. Your child's self-reliance also serves you, because the more he can do for himself, the less energy you have to expend doing things for him.

The Self-Creative Environment

By providing your child with environments in which your intervention in her activities can be kept to a minimum, your child develops greater self-reliance and independence and feels more confident, responsible and free. As a general rule, the more the environment permits your child to do things for himself, without your assistance or intervention, the less frustrated and more self-sufficient he becomes.

Therefore, place things he uses or needs within his reach, to the extent that you can, so he does not require your help to get them. Provide a step he can move about to help him reach things that you cannot place any lower, like the faucet on the sink or the light switch on the wall of his bedroom.

Dangerous Or Inappropriate Objects

If your child finds inappropriate or unsafe objects within his reach, make changes in the environment so that you do not need to incessantly step in. However, keep in mind that everything your child feels drawn to examine provides a learning and developmental experience that takes him to his next higher level. Before removing an object or stopping your child from touching it, see if you can give her an opportunity to examine it safely, perhaps as you keep a hand on it to make sure it does not break or to protect her from injuring herself with it. You might use the object, like a knife, as she watches, to show her the way it works and the safe handling of it.

Introducing Shakespeare, Mozart and Rembrandt

Now more than ever you should be exposing your child to the finest natural and cultural influences. Read to her from the finest books. Place beautiful works of art at her eye level. Play music masterpieces of every genre (keeping the volume at a comfortable level for her sensitive ears). Direct her attention *away* from violent or frightening TV images. Turn off emotionally turbulent music and TV sounds, like people arguing or screaming. Turn off the volume when commercials designed to over-stimulate and hypnotize.

Your Child Is In Love

In the first six years of life, all is new to the child. Do your best to honor your child's innate desire and endless capacity for learning. The sight of a leaf spinning about on a breeze can cause a first plane child to stop in his tracks and gaze with awe for five minutes. It is all new, intriguing and marvelous, like the way you feel when you fall in love. Avoid pushing him to move faster, which may shut off his fascination and block his growing ability to go deeply into life. When he pauses to examine something, let him do so until he feels done. You want to nurture, not stifle, his interest and appreciation.

The Sacred Ceremony Of Self-Creation

As an infant fingers a simple object, such as your keys, or as your toddler practices the execution of a simple act, such as helping you push the stroller down the street, she advances her total development. When you expose her to a kind act, you instill the trait of kindness within her. When you think deeply in her presence, you radiate your pattern of deep mental contemplation and she adopts that power as her own.

Everything the child touches reveals its secrets, feeds her imagination, develops her mastery and understanding of the world. The child under six yearns to expand her intelligence and mastery; she hungers to *become* more. Rather than merely stopping the child from what he wants to do, try to come up with ways that allow him to do what he wants safely and responsibly. For instance, if he wants to hit you, give him a pillow to hit. Excessively blocking the first plane child breeds wild tantrums and discourages him from striving to fulfill his glorious potential.

If we were to truly grasp the vast significance of each moment of a young child's experience, we would observe the child with awe and reverence (as we should), for each moment of experience represents *a sacred ceremony of self-creation.*

Chapter 14
Parenting Ages Six Through Twelve

As the second plane of development begins, your child's "abstract mind" emerges. He now demonstrates a growing ability *and need* to think for himself, and to base his choices on what makes logical sense to him. To achieve this child's cooperation, be willing to explain the reasons behind the rules you expect her to live by.

Forget "Because I Said So"

When your explanation of a rule or direction consists of nothing more than, "Because I said so," you miss a golden opportunity to cultivate your child's capacity to think reasonably. You teach her, in fact, *not* to think before she acts. By showing respect for her thinking ability, you teach her to respect her thinking ability. When you cannot come up with an explanation that satisfies her as to why you want her to do or to not do something, promise to discuss the matter later to help her to understand.

Help him to see how your rules truly serve his best interest. For instance, you might say, "One reason that I want you to speak respectfully to me is that it prepares you to speak respectfully to others. This makes your relationships stronger and more positive, and when you have the help of other people, you can accomplish more in life." You might then give him examples of how disrespectful speech can destroy relationships and cost opportunities.

When he argues against a rule, patiently talk him through the logical consequences of both following and not following the rule. Also, you can help him make different choices by having him think about the impact of his possible choices upon the feelings of other people. While some logical conversation like this may help you with younger children, from the age of six years of age onward it has far more influence.

Watch Out For Your Arguing Habit

During the course of this plane's development the child exhibits a stronger point of view. This may trigger arguing between you. You can save yourself a tremendous amount of pointless stress and strain by staying clear of heated bouts of verbal contention. Do this by disciplining *yourself* not to bicker with your child. Offer your child your point, but don't belabor or force it upon him. If he does not agree with your reasons or your rules, you still need to do what you believe is right.

Don't make being "right" more important than being at peace, loving, kind, respectful, and harmonious with your child. By maintaining a harmonious relationship with your child you evoke her desire to live up to your expectations, to consider feelings, and even to help you out.

Anchoring The Abstract Mind

Children around the age of five or six often experience irrational fears because their imagination surges so strongly at this time that it runs out of control. You help them gain control over their imagination by anchoring it to factual reality. She benefits more by contemplating and exploring the realities that interest her than by indulging in sheer fantasy. This does not mean that fantasy must be totally shunned; only that factuality must be stressed.

Appeal to her fascination with facts of nature and civilization. Talk about the stars, how the ocean "works," why bees buzz. Take her behind the scenes to show her how businesses, artists, government agencies, and farms actually work. If she wants to learn about machines, take her to a machine shop. If he wants to learn about sports, politics, ballet or medicine, take him to places where he can observe the activities that produce the appearances. All of this gets him thinking about how to make his own life work and prepares him for adult responsibility. Constantly look for opportunities to feed his hungry intellect with facts and understanding about the way life is.

Money Matters

Now is the time to begin teaching her about financial responsibility. Give her an allowance and make it her responsibility to make the most of it. Give her opportunities to earn money by connecting her allowance to chores and other responsibilities, like getting good grades in school. Teach her about how debt works and how compound interest makes savvy savers wealthy. If she seems disinterested in money matters, continue trying different approaches until you find a way to bring her into this important dimension of life.

The Issue Of Trust

As the Abstract Mind develops, it enables your child to communicate with more accuracy and detail. This can serve you well, because at the same time, she operates more and more beyond your supervision and control. Now more than ever you begin counting on your child to tell you what is going on, to communicate openly and honestly, so that you can help him to navigate through the increasingly complicated course of his life's journey.

The better your quality of communication with your child, the more open he will be with you. She needs to feel safe, comfortable and secure in your unconditional love, to invite you into the inside story of her life. Children begin lying to their parents when they lose trust in their parents' willingness or ability to love them for who they truly are and to provide the response, guidance, and support they really need.

Discuss Morals

To adhere to a moral code of conduct, your child in the second plane requires a clear understanding of *why* a moral act is superior to an immoral act. Don't be frightened by your child's questioning mind. Be excited about it. It means an opportunity for a new level of bonding and enlightenment has emerged. As you engage in deep conversation about moral issues, you lead your child into deeper, more thoughtful consideration of her choices.

Control And The Internet

The Internet is both liberating and dangerous. Your child's exposure to computer violence or pornography dulls and confuses her sense of appropriate boundaries. Unsupervised chat room conduct can lead your child into the most serious kinds of trouble. You need to be aware of what your child is up to when he is online.

Explain what is appropriate and inappropriate to view *and why*. Explain why *you* need to be aware of what he is doing, and how that does *not* have to be interpreted as your distrust. Then establish boundaries that insure that you are aware of where he hangs out on the Internet.

Rule Respectfully

Your work now and for the rest of your child's development has as much to do with trusting your child's choices as with helping him to make the best choices for himself. This involves a balancing act. You don't want your child to feel that you treat him like a helpless, thoughtless baby. At the same time, you still need to establish certain rules and restrictions. By consistently expressing the highest level of sincere respect for the person your child is, and genuine appreciation for her abilities and potential, you make your rules and restrictions more palatable and achieve cooperation with more harmony and less unhappiness.

Bye, Bye Baby

A major metamorphosis from infancy into childhood has taken place, and how you relate with your child has to reflect that change in order to support your child's fullest development. You may have to frequently remind yourself that your "baby" has been "replaced" by a person who can both handle and benefit from more independence and responsibility.

Treat your child as more grown up and responsible and she will act that way. Parents who complain that their seven-year-old seems to act like a three-year-old ought to look for ways that they contribute to that condition. Perhaps a part of them wants their child to remain their "baby" and looks to the child to continue providing them with that experience.

"My Way"

During this plane, your child's creativity surges. Even if her way seems obviously less efficient to you than your way, giving her the chance to find her own way may, indeed, surprise you as she comes up with a way that you regard as superior to the one you would have imposed upon her. Allowing your child to find his own way of doing things gives him the opportunity to develop competence and confidence.

Encourage Self-Reliance

When your child encounters a problem, say, with school or friends, don't automatically solve it for her; but don't make your child feel abandoned either. Help her to come up with her own reasonable strategies and give her as much responsibility as you can for taking the necessary actions aimed at solving her problems herself.

Standard Responsibilities

Give your second-plane child responsibility for keeping his room clean and his possessions in order, for his personal hygiene, for getting his schoolwork done, for relating respectfully and kindly with other family members. Also, give him responsibility for contributing to the operating of the household by making it his responsibility to do at least one household chore daily.

With your child, compose a list of her weekly responsibilities. Create a second list that includes the privileges she enjoys, including things like watching TV and DVD's, socializing online, riding her bicycle, going to sleepovers. Then, establish the system that in order to preserve her privileges she needs to fulfill her responsibilities. (You will learn ways to support this system in *Part IV*).

Take Preparation Into Account

If your child was not led into the practice of personal responsibility during the previous plane's construction, do not expect her to suddenly be "Little Miss Neatness" now. You may have to be more patient and involved, helping her to develop the skills, strengths and habits needed by joining her in her tasks for a while. You may need to give her lighter responsibilities at first, and gradually build upon that.

The Meaning Of Irresponsible Conduct

When a child of any age slackens off from responsible conduct it often signals that a legitimate need is not being met. You may be expressing too much dissatisfaction and need to spend more time simply enjoying one another's company. Perhaps a disruption in her life, like moving to a new neighborhood or dealing with the arrival of a new sibling, is causing her to lose focus and you need to be more patient and understanding as you gradually restore the daily order of her surroundings and routine. Perhaps she needs you to institute a consequence system on which you follow through to give her the personal incentive and clear sense of your expectations she needs in order to apply more self-discipline.

Don't rely on expressions of frustration, disapproval and disappointment to manipulate your child into more responsible self-conduct. A parent's negative attitude demoralizes and de-motivates a child. Also avoid pinning negative labels onto your child like "lazy," "selfish," "careless," "irresponsible," "slob" as these drive the child to prove them true.

The "Herd Instinct"

The second-plane child experiences a kind of "herd instinct" that drives her to want to feel a part of groups outside the family. Encourage your child to join groups, clubs or teams. One of her primary developmental tasks involves the cultivation of the ability to team with others to achieve a shared goal. The second plane child does not wish to stand out, but rather, to fit in, and now is the time to support her will to conform. She will feel uncomfortable wearing clothes that *you* like if they make her feel like an outsider to the particular group she feels attracted to. Don't worry about her being a follower. At this stage she is learning how to be part of the world community. Her individuality will emerge more assertively in the next stage

Life Outside Reflects Life Inside

Pay attention to the children your second plane child gravitates toward. If you do not like their influence, take a closer look at the quality of your child's life at home. Children gravitate toward individuals who reflect the child's home life ,and they form relationships that reflect the quality of relationships they experience and observe at home. Attempting to establish boundaries regarding whom your child plays with and stays with may actually backfire if you do not simultaneously provide your child with stability, order, and harmonious and respectful relationships at home.

Chapter 15
Parenting Ages Twelve Through Eighteen

Your child enters her third plane of development at around age twelve, and this plane lasts through about her eighteenth year of life. One of your child's primary developmental tasks during this period involves his discovery and assertion of individuality in his quest for a sense of self-importance and self-worth. You support your child in this work by relating to her in a way that makes her feel understood and accepted for who she truly is.

Treat Your Teen
As You Want Your Teen To Be Treated By Others

Think about how you want others to relate with your child and let that guide the way that you relate with him. If you relate in a condescending, disrespectful fashion you prepare your teen to expect and to accept degrading treatment from others. Don't make your respect conditional on performance. Rather, regard your expression of genuine respect for your child as part of your essential contribution to his highest possible level of performance.

This does not mean that you have to condone all that your child chooses to do and allow him to lead his life without your direction. It means that even when you need to establish a boundary or provide corrective feedback, you do it in a manner that preserves his belief in your belief in him.

Rebel With A Cause

The example you set still has an impact on your child's behavior. Your teen respects honesty and authenticity, perhaps above everything else. As you do your best to lead your life in line with your highest values, and honestly face your own shortcomings, your teen will be more open and honest with you, and more receptive. When your teen senses your hypocrisy, she rejects your moral authority and out comes the rebellious urge to behave contrary to what you want her to do.

The Treacherous Teen Years

Your child has never been as powerful as he is now and, to a large extent, his basic personality already has been formed. This leaves you with only about 20% influence over his conduct *at the start of this plane of development*, and your influence gradually diminishes from that point on.

What makes this situation particularly challenging for you is that your child now has the power to make choices with life-long consequences. He may drop out of school. She may get pregnant. He may run away from home and live on the streets. She may become an alcoholic. He may race a car recklessly. She may become ensnared in a gang. He may commit a serious crime. She may pass as an adult and attract more adult opportunities than she can handle. Your child has adult size, strength, and urges with only a child's background of experience and knowledge of the world to guide him. He has never been so at risk of seriously injuring himself and others and you have never been so powerless to protect him from himself.

Worry Does Not Work

With all that is at stake, and with so little power of control, you may feel tempted to worry yourself sick. This often results in being overbearing, hypercritical and suspicious, to the point that the child feels he can do nothing right. This, in turn, causes the child to feel alienated and to reject you and your influence even more than he otherwise would have.

Your teenager does not need you to worry about her. She needs you to believe in her. Discipline yourself *not* to dwell on worrisome thoughts about what your teen is up to and where he may be headed. Think about what you want for your teen and focus on finding ways to constructively contribute toward bringing that about. Look for what your child does right that you can appreciate and admire.

Your teen probably feels far more sensitive and insecure about herself than she lets on. You lower her self-esteem and self-confidence by seeing her and treating her as someone who cannot be trusted. This, in turn, makes her more prone to make choices that match her low expectations of herself.

Responsibility For Adulthood

Your teen's responsible use of his time now provides him with a headstart in his adult years. To help your teenager consider the adult consequences of his choices now, relate with him in an adult fashion. We have traditional ceremonies like Bar and Bat Mitzvahs and Communions that occur during this period; however these have largely suffered a decline into nothing more than superficial excuses for big parties rather than functioning as truly meaningful rites of passage.

Don't wait for your child to act in a more adult fashion before you treat him in a more adult fashion. Give her more adult respect and responsibility *first* as a means of helping her see herself in connection with her adulthood.

Define Responsible Conduct

Think of the teen years as the foundation of adulthood. A primary responsibility of yours consists in doing what you can to prepare your child to handle adult responsibilities. Do this by relating with him in a more adult fashion and by treating his chores at home and his performance at school as his "job," backed up by consequences involving a restriction of privileges for irresponsible conduct. As your child progresses through this plane, your power to restrict privileges diminishes to the point that all you can really restrict is what you do for your child. Don't expect consequences to work, though, if you:

- Routinely express an angry, critical attitude toward your child
- Treat her as one unworthy of your love, trust, confidence or respect
- Provide her with poor role modeling
- Surround her with a chaotic, inharmonious, conflict-ridden home

In addition to household chores, require him to devote a portion of his time to some form of community service. You can join him in this for a powerful and positive form of bonding. In the summer, if he is not in summer school, let him have a two-week vacation after school ends, and a one-week vacation before school starts up again. Between those breaks, require him to work at a job, or to do community service, during normal school hours. An exception to this would be a long family trip of some kind. Also require a certain amount of summer academic work (consult his teachers for guidance here).

Don't Be A Parent Drop-Out

Children are more likely to drop out of school when their parents drop out of their children's school life. By involving yourself in your child's school life, including attending regular meetings with teachers and participating in the P.T.A., you increase the likelihood that your child will take her school life more seriously.

Tuning Out

If your teen tunes you out, it very likely indicates that you tuned her out first. When you speak to her, you may not really be paying attention to how your words, tones and attitudes impact her. You may have fallen into the habit of criticizing and complaining or arguing too much. You may not be "tuning in" sufficiently to how she really feels, or really listening to what she says.

How To Reach Your Teen

To reach your teen, *you* need to make the effort. Even if he rejects you, continue trying and don't give up. Keep working on making a positive connection with him by scheduling time together and doing your best to make that time a satisfying experience for you both.

Find out what your child wants to do with you, and do your best to do that rather than imposing upon your child what you want to do. Share in his experiences by going to his games or even just watching as he paints, as she dances, as he plays a game of catch with a friend. The more you lovingly participate in your child's life, the more your child will allow you in.

Be Non-Defensive

Listen to your child. Let *her* reach *you*. If she tells you that you act like you never made a mistake, take that to mean that you need to express yourself in a more human, humble manner. If you fear admitting your mistakes, admit *that*. You may be amazed at how forgiving and understanding your child can be when you let your guard down, and how that encourages her to be more open and honest with you, and how that builds a positive bond between you that makes her *want* to do her best.

Pay very close attention to recognize when you become defensive. If your teen says something like, "You never listen to me," resist the urge to argue, "Of course I do." Instead, accept the feedback and pay closer attention to how you actually do relate with her. If you build a wall of defensiveness that blocks out your teen's messages, you can expect your teen to do the same to you.

When Teens Withdraw

Teens experience more extreme emotions and mood swings than they have ever felt. When you cannot satisfy your teen by giving her the decision she wants, she may feel overwhelmed by her emotional reaction and feel the need to withdraw for a while into her own space. When he is going through a tough time with friends or with school, he may want to withdraw out of feelings of shame or guilt. Regard your teen's withdrawal as a sign that he needs some help in dealing with his strong feelings.

Give your teen privacy and space when he wants it, but check in frequently to see if she feels ready to come together again. Try to come up with something the two of you can do together to help him to relax and open up. Definitely do not carry around a grudge and wait for your teen to come to you. *Be the bigger person.* Don't engage in a contest of who can care less.

Do Not Argue

Make every effort to understand your teen's point of view and to empathize with his feelings. Let him think his thoughts and have his say. At the end of any discussion in which he tries to get you to change a rule or decision, however, do what you believe is right and be willing to help him to understand your reasons.

If the two of you have a history of arguing, establish the ground rules for discussion. "The basic rule is that we must speak kindly and respectfully with one another even when we totally disagree with one another's point of view. When that fails to happen, we take a time out and return to the conversation later."

Teen Idols

While the first plane child automatically wants to be like whoever happens to be around him, the teenager finds a particular idol as a role model to emulate, someone who expresses the qualities that he wants to possess. Children exposed to negative role models look up to individuals who lead them down troublesome roads. Do your best to expose your child to positive role models, individuals who inspire her with courage and good will. Avoid criticizing him for not feeling inspired by someone who inspires you. Pay attention to your child in order to get a sense of the kind of person he truly wants to be: a leader, an actor, an adventurer, a public servant. Then seek out individuals who express qualities that ignite his passion to pursue a great destiny, and introduce them to your teen.

Chapter 16
Parenting Ages Eighteen
Through Twenty-Four

While your legal responsibility has ended, you continue to have a role in your "child's" development during the time they are ages eighteen through twenty-four. It consists of applying the finishing touches of launching your offspring into complete responsibility for himself.

The Emptying Nest

Just as your young adult "child" now moves into independent self-reliance, so do you. Be prepared for the diminution of your significance, involvement, and influence in your "child's" life. Focus more now on leading your own life meaningfully and, if you feel challenged by the change, focus on coming to terms with your emptying nest. Some parents unwittingly foster their young adult "child's" continuing dependence out of fear of losing the purpose or the power of having a "child" to raise. This often lies at the root of the parent's belief in the helplessness or incompetence of her "child."

To help you to let go, seek out a new purpose for yourself at the start of this period. If you love children, find ways to serve the children of your community. If you do not know what to do that could ever feel as satisfying and as important as raising your child, then make your new purpose the search for a new purpose. In the beginning, the journey may seem dark and dreadful; but gradually it will brighten as you see ways to make your new freedom an exciting and fulfilling chapter of life.

Hear Their Calling

During the construction of this plane of development, the young adult awakens to the person she truly is and the role she wants to play in life. He discovers his mission, his calling, his vision of life that satisfies his sense of purpose. Your "child" must follow this inner directive to find any real happiness or meaningful success. Make no effort to dissuade or to discourage your young adult from the life she chooses to live.

Offer your advice when asked for. If you think that he might make a choice that more closely aligns with the person he truly is, let him know; but if he holds fast to his belief, be supportive and encouraging of his decision. If he seeks your counsel, share your practical wisdom as to how he might proceed to make his dream a reality. If she wants your financial support, give within your means but base your support on the contingency that she apply herself responsibly.

Rules Of Respect And Responsibility

Your fourth plane "child" has surpassed your power to influence through the consequence of privilege restriction beyond the three most basic ones:

- The privilege of living in your home
- The privilege of receiving your financial aid or support
- The privilege of having a direct relationship with you

Make these contingent upon your "child's" demonstration of:

- Respectful kindness and consideration in his mode of relating with you
- Genuine commitment, demonstrated by action, to taking full responsibility for himself

Don't expect your "child" to accept responsibility for himself as long as you give him no responsibility for doing so. If she demands the freedom to do exactly as she pleases without regard to her responsibilities or the impact of her choices on the other members of the household, she needs to live on her own. If he insists on treating you poorly, on taking advantage of your kindness and generosity, or on posing a threat to your safety or possessions, he loses the right to be in a direct relationship with you – he gets a major "time-out."

Some "Unacceptable" Examples

As long as your "child" lives under your roof, make it unacceptable for him to, say, not pick up after himself around the house; not to contribute to the household chores; come and go as he pleases (without letting you know when you can expect him); require you to be able to sleep in peace at night while he stays out all hours (particularly without calling); demand that you drop everything and run when he wants something from you. If your "child" demonstrates values that you find intolerable, you do not need to tolerate them now. If she shows a lack of respect toward any household member or a lack of responsibility by dropping out of school *and* work, have a couple of discussions about your issues in which you make clear your expectations *and the consequence for not meeting them.*

Give The Gift Of Not Giving Too Much

Regard living with you and receiving your financial support as privileges, not rights, that must be earned. Do not deprive your young-adult "child" of the character-building experience of independent self-reliance when he stops demonstrating responsibility for himself or respect for your feelings and values. As in the early years, doing too much for a "child" undermines her will to do enough for herself.

PART FOUR

YOUR CHILD-DISCIPLINE OPTIONS

Chapter 17
Your Child-Discipline Options

Parents are often far too interested in the use of "time-out" when it comes to child discipline. What we need to be far more concerned with is the quantity and quality of "time-in."

Time-In

In order for your child to give you her best behavior, she needs you to spend enough time with her. How much time is enough? It varies with every child.

As a general rule for the best results, at least one parent should spend all day long, nearly every day, with a child under three. For a child age three to age six, at least one parent should spend a minimum of five hours of waking time five days a week, and all day and evening on the weekends. The parent who functions as a secondary caregiver should be spending about four hours a day of waking time with the child during the week, and about twice that on weekends. For two parent households, the family should be spending as much time as possible together as a whole during these crucial, formative years. As the child advances beyond the first plane of development, the amount of needed time-in with parents gradually diminishes.

When a child spends too little time with a parent, the child's level of morale and motivation drop, and the drive to behave in less cooperative, less considerate ways kicks in. This is a reality you cannot change. Your heart will tell you when your child needs to be with you. If you cannot satisfy that need, be more patient, tolerant, understanding and compassionate in your handling of her behavior.

Quality Time

Additionally, you need to insure that 95% of the time you spend with your child is a positive, harmonious, loving, satisfying experience for both of you. This requires that you learn how to lead your child in a way that she wants to follow the vast majority of the time (Child Discipline Option 3). When her behavior displeases you, make it your primary responsibility to maintain your peace and poise. Make it your responsibility to adapt to his personality so that you maintain your deep, loving connection.

The 95% Rule

Making sure that 95% of the time you and your child spend together is harmonious quality time represents one side of what I call "The 95% rule." The other side involves directing your attention, thought and speech to focus 95% of the time on what you want and on what you appreciate, and no more than 5% on what you do not like and do not want. If you direct more than 5% of your attention, time and energy into concern about what you do not like or do not want, you begin exuding a negative attitude that your child picks up, causing her to feel more defensive and resistant.

In keeping with this 95% rule, avoid making a big deal over your child's mistakes. Reacting with emotional intensity to your child's behavior unbalances you and your relationship, generating more conflict, not more cooperation. Your emotional reactions constitute a use of your energy. You give too much energy, and therefore power, to a behavior you wish to discourage when you react with emotional intensity against it. Do, however, make a big deal out of displays that you like and appreciate. Receiving your expressions of appreciation, love, gratitude, and approval fuels your child's drive to do even better. If you do not see what your child does well or right, you are not looking. Seek and you will find.

Practicing the 95% rule will keep you and your child feeling positive and functioning constructively, and it provides the necessary foundation for any Child Discipline Option to work well.

Correct Correction

Constructive child-discipline leads a child toward demonstrating and developing responsible self-discipline without injuring the child's feelings of self-confidence or self-worth. Destructive child-discipline corrects incorrectly by attempting to manipulate or to dominate the child in a way that leaves the child feeling abandoned, disgraced or powerless. It involves the use of hitting, shaming, yelling, issuing verbal put-downs, punitive "lock-ups" (extended "time-outs"), withdrawing of love, and blaming the child for the parent's feelings of frustration, impatience, unhappiness, powerlessness or disappointment.

Destructive child discipline focuses too much on controlling the child's immediate behavior at all costs. Constructive child discipline establishes boundaries in a way that honors the sacred bond between parent and child. Constructive child discipline is based on cooperation, peace, and love, while destructive discipline is based on fighting, anger and stress.

From Essentials To Options

If the following Child Discipline Options produce disappointing results, reexamine your child's overall life-situation in the light of what you have read up to this point to identify those essential areas of your child's life that may need work. At the same time, consider the fact that nothing you do will give you absolute and immediate control over your child's behavior. Your child's behavior, like your own, can only improve by small degrees at a time. You sometimes need to be willing to tolerate unwanted behavior for a while as you employ a strategy aimed at producing gradual improvement.

You Have Five Options

Constructive child-discipline can be boiled down to involve the use of five basic options. In the chapters that follow we will examine them in detail. Below is a brief summary of each. When you encounter a problem with your child's behavior, review the follow-ing list of Child Discipline Options in the order they are presented here and choose the Option that seems to best suit your situation at the time.

Option One: Conscious Detachment We can describe this as intentionally overlooking a behavior. Your Option of least effort, you apply this by deliberately *not* responding to something your child does. Use it to avoid overly controlling your child and to dis-courage your child from seeking your attention or involvement through unwanted behavior.

Option Two: Natural Consequences This is similar to your first Option, but it involves allowing your child to experience more unpleasantness than your not reacting. Here, you let the unpleasant consequences that naturally follow your child's choice of actions teach her to choose differently.

Option Three: Building When you do take action, this should be your choice *the vast majority of the time.* It consists of *building* or strengthening your positive bond with your child by using positive, loving *connection* in your way of direction and correction.

Option Four: Guiding Choices To apply this Option, you substitute your child's unacceptable choice with two choices that you approve of. This satisfies the child's healthy and natural need for freedom, power and control, while you responsibly limit her choic-es. In actual practice, many find this Option a bit unwieldy and largely ineffective, but it is worth a try.

Option Five: Negative Consequences This represents your last resort and most unpleasant Option. It entails the establishing of a boundary in a firm, consistent manner. It may involve you restrict-ing your child's privileges as a consequence. Employ this rarely, no more than once or twice a day. If applied correctly, your warnings will do the job and you will rarely need to follow through.

Consider Your Options Before Responding

Your five basic Options follow a logical sequence, with the first being the easiest and least aggressive, and the last being the most demanding and assertive. When you believe that your child's behavior requires your direction or redirection, pause *before* reacting to consider these Options in the sequence presented above.

You will have to rely on your own best judgment to determine which Option best suits your present challenge. This requires your practice of peace and poise when making a decision, because peace and poise constitute your most resourceful, competent mode of operating.

Don't expect to always know exactly what will succeed. Sometimes you have to patiently experiment and give an Option a reasonable amount of time to work. How long should you wait? Again, this is entirely a matter of your best judgment.

Forget Discipline "Magic"

No child-discipline system in existence provides instant and absolute control over a child's behavior. Don't demand that kind of control or you craze yourself (though it seems your child drives you crazy). Your relationship with your child is a *human* relationship, meaning you have to face the limitations of your power and your responsibility to grow into a more loving, humble, understanding human being. The best you can do is to make the best use of the power you have, and that is what a clear idea of these Options equips you to do. These Options provide you with all the leverage you have *and all the leverage you really need* to fulfill your parental responsibility and help your child to feel and to do her very best. With practice, you will find these Options easier to use, and more effective to use for increasingly satisfying results.

Chapter 18
Option One: Conscious Detachment

Beginning around the age of twelve-months, a child demonstrates the gradually growing capacity to change her behavior in response to consequences. The child's achievement of the results he pursues through a given behavior encourages him to repeat that behavior for those results. When that child's behavior fails to produce the results she is after, she loses her incentive to repeat that behavior. We can call this governing principle of child behavior *"The Law Of Results."* We can illustrate it in the form of the following equations:

THE LAW OF RESULTS
Behavior + Desired Results = Encouragement Of That Behavior
Behavior – Desired Results = Discouragement Of That Behavior

The Law Of Results In Action
If your child yells at you to get your attention, giving him your attention when he yells – even when you turn to him with a request or a demand that he stop yelling – teaches him to yell *because his yelling got your attention.* We used to believe that expressing much anger or frustration in reaction to a child's unwanted behavior would automatically discourage that behavior; but now we know that even your fierce demand to *"Stop that right now!"* makes her feel like the center of your attention and satisfies her with the sense of power that she desires. Thus, while your intensely aggressive reaction may discourage her on one level, it encourages her on another level, so that you work at cross-purposes against yourself.

If your child can cause you to become upset by, say, repeatedly asking you for something after you tell her "No," you encourage her to repeat that behavior by losing your composure in response to it. To assert control over you, your child might use obnoxious, dangerous or destructive behavior. If you seem unfazed by that behavior, he sees that it fails to achieve the result he is after. Based on The Law Of Results, this may prove adequate to successfully discourage him from repeating that manipulative tactic.

You may use Conscious Detachment successfully to teach your child that you do not respond to whining; that nagging does not control you; that making obnoxious sounds or monstrous faces produces no affect upon you; that disrespectful speech, tantrums, ignoring your directions, or making endless demands does *not* get him the control that he is after.

"I Want What I Don't Want"

Children sometimes use their behavior to ensnare a parent's draining involvement. She might, for instance, demand a particular food for dinner; but as soon as you serve it, she demands something else. This "game" continues until you stop "playing." You might end the game by calmly stating in a no-nonsense tone something like: "I have offered you all of the choices I am going to offer." If she asks again, you can state, again in a no-nonsense, nonplussed manner, "I gave you my decision. You can eat what you have before you or pass on dinner." If she asks again, you might use Conscious Detachment by simply ignoring her demands and acting like they have no effect on you.

"Follow–The–Leader"

Your child may deliberately engage in a series of little missteps to keep you focused on his every move. First he slides a magazine off the coffee table. When you correct that, he picks up the remote control and begins pressing buttons (in more ways than one). When you correct that, he gives the dog's tail a tug. This game of "follow-the-leader" continues as long as you continue to play. If you react with negative emotion, the situation only deteriorates.

To end this game, *before you react* to a behavior or to a demand, pause to ask yourself if a better alternative might be to appear to ignore the behavior and to give no response. By asserting control *over your reaction*, you become the leader. Control over a situation begins with controlling your reaction to the situation.

Does your child use screaming, crying, creating a mess, ignoring your directions, or other forms of disturbing behavior *to get your goat*? If you interpret this to be happening, it can easily trigger your angry response. Your angry reaction, though, increases your suffering and contributes to a worsening of the child's behavior. By demonstrating the self-control needed to not give your child "your goat," you enjoy more inner peace, while withholding from your child the power over you that she may be after.

The Conscious Detachment Attitude

Conscious Detachment applied as a means of discouraging unwanted behavior functions consistently with the 95% Rule as it avoids making a big deal over unwanted behavior. Remember that intense emotional reactions to a problem expand the problem. Therefore, even when you need to take more assertive action, maintain the attitude of Conscious Detachment toward behavior you do not want to encourage. Thus, you make the most of what you want and the least of what you don't want.

Beyond Conscious Detachment

Conscious Detachment is not *always* appropriate. Sometimes a parent's expression of deep concern in response to a problem-behavior gives the child the sense of value and importance she needs to make better choices. You want to avoid making too much or too little of a behavior you wish to change. In each instance, with each child, you need to pay close attention to the child to gain a sense of your reaction's impact upon the child.

To effectively direct and redirect your child, you need to understand what he is up to. You may need to patiently observe your child and consider the situation and your options for a while before responding. (This actually represents a form of Conscious Detachment because while you are observing, you are not reacting.) You may never come up with a strategy for effectively handling a particular behavior. In that case, you would be applying Conscious Detachment by default and find that, in conjunction with the child's maturation process and your application of your best parenting skills possible, your child's behavior seemingly improves on its own.

When Nothing Is Enough

When there seems to be nothing you can do to satisfy your child, nothing may be all that it will take. In other words, when you cannot seem to meet your child's demands, making no further efforts to do so may prove to be your most effective response. Beyond this, there exists a definite limit to how much reacting and controlling you can engage in. Every effort you make to control your child expends your energy. When you feel fatigued, you have less energy to draw upon, and you may need to tolerate instead of control until your batteries recharge. Not reacting is a way of letting up on yourself. If you do not let up, you may make yourself sick and drift into a negative zone.

Are You Too Controlling?

Most of us have automatic reaction habits that drive us to control more than we can and more than we need to. Sometimes we feel the burden of having to fix *everything*. The next time you feel that way, take it as a sign that you are trying to fix too much.

Emotional reactions fool us into believing that something that really does not matter very much matters way too much to overlook. As a general rule, regard your automatic emotional reaction as misleading. If you calm down and consider the situation a little longer, you will find that your best response is almost always based on peace and poise. Before seeking control, particularly if you feel the least bit of stress or strain, pause to consider letting things work out a little longer on their own.

Conserve Your Energy

In the chapter on *The G.A.T.E. Of Self Control,* we discussed the paramount importance of conserving your energy. Spending too much effort correcting things that don't need your control deprives you of the energy you need to adequately handle more important challenges that do require more active involvement. Applying Conscious Detachment saves you from getting caught up in the stressful habit of micromanaging your child, which equates to making too much of the annoying but insignificant displays of natural behavior and testing. It also gives your child the break from being corrected and controlled that she might need. Deliberately appearing to overlook a child's behavior, or Conscious Detachment, requires zero effort, beyond the effort it takes to maintain your peace and poise.

Things May Escalate Before Improving

Be prepared for the possibility that ignoring your child's obnoxious manipulation tactic may cause him to step up the intensity of his efforts. If that occurs, *don't react hastily.* Your continued non-reactivity may prove sufficient to lead him to the conclusion that his attempts to control you this way have no chance of succeeding. However, if his reaction continues to escalate, consider your other Child-Discipline Options presented in the following chapters. Conscious Detachment is not always the answer, but often it is. Keep that in mind the next time that you feel the urge to take control.

Chapter 19
Option Two: Natural Consequences

While children learn from the example we set for them from the very beginning of life (through The Law Of Reflection), they learn from results (The Law Of Results) only as they develop the cognitive and physical capacity to do so. Until your child develops the capacity to recognize the relationship between his actions and the consequences, and demonstrates the ability to alter his behavior accordingly, you have the responsibility to protect him from harmful choices he might otherwise make for himself. However, you do your child a disservice by overly insulating him from life's educational experiences.

Your second Child-Discipline Option, the use of Natural Consequences, is slightly more assertive and certainly more unpleasant than your first Option, yet it still involves no direct action on your part. You employ this Option by allowing your child to learn from the unpleasant consequence that his action brings upon himself. You may usually begin using Natural Consequences effectively by the child's age of three, perhaps even a little earlier. *Use this consequence only when you feel certain that your child can benefit from the lesson of her experience.*

Making Life Your Parenting Ally
By deliberately *not* intervening when, say, your child plays too roughly with one of his breakable toys, you allow the Natural Consequence of his breaking the toy to teach him to handle his things more carefully. You may issue one or two warnings beforehand, such as, "Playing that way with that toy can break it." After that, you might allow him to learn from the experience he brings upon himself. You may clarify the lesson afterwards by explaining

what happened: "Your toy broke because you played too roughly with it." When you use Natural Consequences properly, you make life your parenting ally by letting experience teach your child.

Teaching Responsibility

As we explored in the previous chapter, stepping in to guide or direct your child may not always be your best option. Sometimes, allowing a child to go through the Natural Consequences of his behavior proves to be the best way to teach him to take responsibility for himself. For instance, you might permit your daughter to boss her friends around (as long as you observe no real abuse happening) to the point that *they* decide to leave. Then, her experience of their choosing to not play with her teaches her how to relate with others. Another example might be to *not* remind your child to bring his book bag to school, even as you agonize while you watch him leaving home without it. Thus, you count on the Natural Consequence of his school experience to be his best teacher.

How Harsh Is Too Harsh?

Using Natural Consequences requires you to be strong enough to allow your child to pass through some degree of frustration or disappointment *for her own good.* Allowing a child to experience too much of this does not help her to be more responsible. No fixed system of measurements applies here, beyond the obvious forms of neglect that would endanger a child. For some children, at certain times, the lesson of breaking a toy through rough treatment may deliver a constructive lesson *even if you were to immediately purchase a replacement.* However, for other children or at other times, to purchase a replacement would only "rescue" the child right out of his constructive life-education. You need to rely on your own best judgment to determine what works best with your child at any given time. If you feel uncertain, experiment with milder forms of guidance before moving on to sterner measures.

The School Of Life

Your child's school education is important, but so is his life-education. Earnest's parents understood this. Earnest had been saving money for months to purchase a special collector's baseball card. He even marked on his calendar the day he would have enough money to buy it. While out with his mother one week before that day arrived, he noticed a new set of shin guards to wear with roller blades that he wanted.

His mother reminded him that he already had shin guards in perfectly good condition. She also communicated that if he purchased these, he would not have enough to buy the baseball card he had been saving up for. He said that he didn't care. She knew that he would care very much, and she wanted to stop him from spending his money on impulse, but she did not do so.

When the day arrived when he would have been able to purchase the card but could not, he begged his parents to buy it for him. They really wanted to, because he seemed so unhappy and disappointed. Instead, they controlled *themselves* and allowed their child to learn about responsible money-management from the unpleasant Natural Consequences of his choices.

Chapter 20
Option Three: Building

When you deem it appropriate to take some form of action aimed at directing your child's behavior, use your third Child-Discipline Option, Building, 95% of the time. Building consists of re-directing or correcting in a way that *builds* upon the loving bond between you. To direct your child's behavior with Building, you sort of *please* your child into or out of a behavior so that your child may not even notice herself being directed or corrected. Building makes responsible parenting easier and more enjoyable.

Reverence: The Ultimate Building Attitude

When you feel the least bit frustrated or irritated with your child's behavior, immediately stop trying to control him and focus on your most sacred depth of positive feeling for your child. Your reverential appreciation of your child, giving your thanks to God for your child's very being, reaches your child at the core, inspiring him to give you his finest behavior.

Building Tactics

Directing your child's behavior through Building consists of employing one of the following positive Building Tactics:

- Joining
- Assisting
- Praising Or Thanking In Advance
- Purposeful Play
- Positive Substitution
- Subtle Distraction
- Building On Strengths

Joining

When you join a child in a harmonious, loving way, the feeling of loving connection inspires the child to behave in a more loving and considerate way. When you wish to improve your child's behavior, instead of overtly directing, try to just join with your child in a pleasant way. You might try hugging him instead of asking him to settle down. When he begins to behave in an inappropriate manner, you might try just sitting close to him with harmonious, peaceful feelings or begin doing something with him that he likes. This often ends the unwanted behavior without the slightest stress or strain.

Join In Responsible Action

You can also use *joining* to eliminate your child's resistance to performing a responsible activity. If your child resists doing a household chore, like taking out the trash, offer to join him as he does the chore. If your child refuses to pick up his toys, to clean his room, to go to the kitchen to get his own cup of milk, to walk the dog or change the cat's litter box, to do her homework or to make his bed, offer to join her while she does it.

When she accepts your offer, make yourself pleasant, harmonious company. You do not make your child's responsible behavior too easy on him by joining him in the act. You provide her with essential quality time that in and of itself supports the child's natural desire to behave responsibly. Don't worry that your child will depend upon you more. You can gradually extricate yourself as he develops the habit of fulfilling each responsibility.

Assisting

Assisting your child in the performance of a responsible action means going beyond simply joining him. Here, you actually do some of the work yourself—sometimes much of the work or, occasionally, all of the work—as she looks on. For instance, if your child resists taking out the trash even after you offer to keep him company, offer to carry the trash out yourself if he will keep *you* company. When he accepts this offer, be sure that you perform the task with a positive attitude. (Do you see how this models responsible motivation?)

In terms of having your child do the chore for you, this approach seems to be of no value. However, it does serve to get your child to exercise some degree of self-discipline in the direction of personal responsibility, which acts as a stepping-stone on which you can *build* further progress. Gradually, you can turn more and more over to your child. Also, while you work together, or while your child watches you do the work, the competencies you exhibit rub off on your child based on The Law Of Reflection. Have your child pay close attention to you as you perform each step of the operation. For instance, while you help him make the bed, have him watch your every move. It will then be easier for him to repeat your moves and fulfill his responsibility of making his bed more quickly and easily, thus defusing his resistance to doing so.

Remember that your purpose in assisting is not to relieve your child of responsibility. Rather, it is to lead her into the self-discipline of fulfilling more responsibility. Offer no more assistance than is necessary and withdraw your assistance (not necessarily your company) as her willingness and competence increase.

Praising Or Thanking In Advance

When you want your child to do something, try praising and thanking her for doing it *in advance*. This tactic exhibits an uncanny power to bring out desirable behavior that has not yet happened. For instance, to encourage him to pick up after himself, try sincerely praising him for picking up after himself and genuinely thanking him for the contribution *before he has done so*. To encourage your child to play nicely with others at the playground, right before you launch her into activity you might say, "I want to thank you very much for playing so nicely with the other children at the playground today."

Purposeful Play

This is one of the most effective uses of Building to use with younger children, and the one that I personally use most often. Purposeful Play means turning what you want your child to do into a form of play that your child wants to participate in. For instance, you might encourage her to leave the playground when you want by challenging her to race you to the car. Using humor often makes the play even more effective. In this case you might say, "And as we race we have to cluck loudly like a chicken!" Your child will likely laugh as you do this. Then, the next time that you turn a direction into a form of play, she will have a conscious or subconscious expectation of enjoying the experience and feel more prompted to cooperate. At the same time, using humor and play keeps you feeling happier, more positive, more successful and more energized.

If your child refuses to clean up his mess, you might use Purposeful Play by singing a cleanup song or by turning cleaning up into a sort of "basketball game" in which you each take a turn at tossing a toy into the toy bin. You can count aloud or use a timer to challenge your child to beat the clock in a game of "Room-Cleaning Olympics." You can tickle her all the way upstairs to her room for bed. Parents of infants apply this method when they pretend a spoonful of hot cereal is like an airplane flying food into their child's mouth.

Positive Substitution

Routinely blocking a child from doing or having what he wants triggers the child's frustration and aggression while teaching the child, by example, to be oppositional. Using Positive Substitution represents a constructive alternative to blocking by providing the child with an acceptable substitute that satisfies her. For instance, if she wants to throw a wooden block in the house, give her something soft and harmless to throw, like a ball of socks or take her outside and invite her to throw sticks at the trees. Thus, she gets to do what she wants while behaving appropriately. If he wants to go outside when you cannot allow that, offer to help him to build something with his blocks. If she wants to handle a breakable object, don't just snatch it away. Place something else in her hands that she may delight in.

Subtle Distraction

This works primarily with children under six. When your child engages in whining or nagging, or demands to do something that you cannot allow, use a form of distraction to defuse the situation. You might suddenly say, "Hey, can you do this?" and spin around three times very quickly. If he does that, come up with something else, and continue until you can easily lead him out of the unwanted activity.

Be imaginative in your application of this tricky method. For instance, when he insists on having his cup refilled so that he can spill more water on the floor, you might suddenly invite him to join you in another room to see something "really interesting." When you arrive there, point to anything at all, like a chair, and say, "Now isn't that chair interesting!" Then you can turn the whole thing into a game by saying, "Listen. It's singing." When she laughs, you have successfully distracted her.

Rely Upon Strengths

Instead of harping on your child's faults or weak-points, focus on his gifts, strengths, and talents on a ratio of about 95% positive to 5% negative. As a result, your child's self-confidence *builds*, helping him to go outside of his comfort zone. For instance, if your child exhibits a naturally kind and gentle nature, but lacks confidence when it comes to participating in group activities, don't push him to be more of a joiner. Instead, you might find a way to build upon his strength, by, say, joining him in feeding the hungry or in bringing toys to hospitalized children. If he acts out in class for laughs, you might help him to develop and rely on his natural talent by signing him up for an acting class. The better he feels about himself the more inclined he will be to take the risk of expanding his horizons.

Building Works

Some may argue that Building is too soft on a child. "Children don't need to be harmonized with; they need to be controlled" or "Children need to do what you want whether they want to or not," they believe. However, you will find that those who express such beliefs exhibit problems with feelings. They do not feel very happy, loving, content, or grateful and they do not trust others enough to open up intimately. They probably feel quite resentful toward their children and harbor a condescending attitude that regards the child as responsible for that, not taking responsibility for how that attitude affects the child. They "believe in" using angry yelling to dominate, in working so hard that the work has no meaning and in working with a negative attitude; they "believe in" in arguing to make other's wrong and in saying cruel things that hurt others feelings. They believe in complaining and in blaming their feelings of frustration, disappointment, futility, and even rage on others – even on an infant. They don't criticize you harshly because they have a criticism problem; they criticize you because you "make" them angry with you, because they see everyone but themselves as responsible for their happiness. Thus, they are without a doubt depressed. If you want that, then Building is *not* for you.

The purpose of Building is to lead your child in way that works consistently with the 95% Rule, which, you may recall, states that for a child to give you his best behavior, 95% of the time you spend together needs to be harmonious and mutually satisfying. Building works because it helps your child avoid developing inappropriate behavior habits while helping him to form appropriate habits. It works because it turns the rigorous job of keeping your child's behavior on track into a more pleasant, positive experience.

Building will not always be the response to choose, but 95% of the time, if you deem your first two Options too passive, Building is the one to use. However, 5% of the time you need to be ready, willing and able to resort to one of the firmer Options that follow.

Chapter 21
Option Four: Guiding Choices

Guiding Choices is your fourth Child-Discipline Option. It represents the beginning of strictness. Consider using it when the more passive Options of Conscious Detachment and Natural Consequences, and the positive Option of Building, either fail to work or seem too "soft" for the situation. You may begin using this Option effectively with children starting around the age of three-years-old, when they exhibit the ability to comprehend it.

Limit Your Child's Choices

To apply Guiding Choices, when your child wants to do something that you cannot allow, offer him two choices that you can allow. Thus, you satisfy your child's natural desire for autonomy, at least to some degree, while keeping her behavior on track. For instance, if your child demands to stay up a little later at bedtime, you can give her the choice of going to bed right now with a story, or going to bed in ten minutes without a story. If she rejects both choices, try simply repeating your offer.

If your child wants to purchase something she sees on the shelf, and you don't want to spend that much money, you might apply this method by offering her a choice between two items within your budget. If she insists on the overly expensive item, inform her that is not an option by saying something like, "Choose between these two or we purchase nothing."

The Choice Of Building

When your child resists doing something that you want, consider using this Option in conjunction with Building. For instance, if your child resists cleaning her room, give her the choice of doing it with your help (the Building Options of Joining and Assistance) or doing it on her own. Let's say that your child resists getting dressed when you need to leave in the morning. You might offer, "Do you want to dress yourself right now or would you like us to play the getting-dressed-right-now game?" If he chooses the latter, you need to come up with a way of turning the process into a form of play that he enjoys. If your child resists washing his hands before coming to the dinner table, you might say, "Do you want to wash your hands on your own right now, or would you like me to join you and we can wash our hands together right now?"

When Your Child Rejects Both Choices

If your child refuses your choices, you can repeat your offer one time. If he continues rejecting your options and insisting on his first choice, calmly and patiently consider the use of your Conscious Detachment, Building or the following, final Option, Negative Consequences.

Chapter 22
Option Five: Negative Consequences (Your Last Resort)

Use your Negative Consequence Option only as a last resort, and no more than 5% of the time, as your method of guiding your child's behavior. If you use this Option more than that, you foster an atmosphere of contention in your relationship with your child that incites more opposition. Employ it calmly and confidently, without anger or stress.

While you will probably find it to be the least pleasant of your Options, it remains, nonetheless, an integral aspect of parenting with love, as it provides a child with a clear understanding of what is expected of her and sufficient motivation to do her best. There is nothing "wrong" with your child because you have to occasionally resort to this firmest of Options, so don't resent him when it becomes necessary to employ it. And don't fear that using it will make your child love you less. The child who is not held accountable does not feel that she really counts.

How It Works

This Option consists of using a Negative Consequence (something your child does not want to experience) to discourage your child from engaging in an undesired behavior or to encourage your child to choose a desired behavior. In essence, using this Option communicates to your child, "If you want X you need to do Y." A typical example of this would be, "If you want your desert, you must first eat your meal."

Choose as the Negative Consequence the timed restriction of one or more of your child's privileges – things your child likes but does not need. As a general rule, give your child two clear warnings that a Negative Consequence will follow if he does not cooperate. If you know what the Negative Consequence will be, inform him of it. When used properly, you will only *at most* have to issue one or two warnings a few times during any given day and your warnings will prove sufficient nearly all of the time, so that you will rarely need to follow through.

Twelve Of The Most Common Mistakes

This method proves highly effective for gaining immediate cooperation *when used correctly*. If it does not work for you, then most likely one or more of the following twelve common mistakes that parents make has something to do with it:

- You spend too little harmonious quality time with your child
- You over-rely on the Negative Consequence Option (using it too often)
- You express too much anger and dissatisfaction in reaction to your child's behavior
- Your mode of relating with your child hurts her feelings too deeply (causing the child to feel humiliated, embarrassed, shunned, belittled, or unsure of your love)
- There may be something troubling going on in your child's life that makes it impossible for her to live up to your expectations – something you need to address (such as too much chaos, contention, instability, change, or unhappiness in her surroundings)
- You restrict privileges that your child does not care about
- You fail to follow through consistently enough (so that your warnings carry no weight)
- You impose such severe consequences that you end up hardening your child and stoking the flame of his rebellion
- Your child is too young or developmentally impaired to comprehend or constructively respond to the consequence of her

action
- Someone continues modeling for your child the very behavior you are attempting to discourage
- The child feels threatened or has had his boundaries violated in some way
- You use hitting, yelling, issuing verbal put-downs, emotional complaining, or the display of intimidating emotional blowups to control your child

You Need To Know Your Child

For any given child, at any given time, a different Negative Consequence will work best. If you select overly harsh consequences, you incite rebellion and stiffer resistance and may even cause physical or emotional harm. On the other hand, if your consequences are too mild for your child, your child will brush them off. As a general rule, use the mildest form of discipline possible to satisfy the needs of the situation and be willing to experiment.

The privilege you restrict needs to match your child's likes and dislikes. Removing the privilege of playing with a toy that your child could care less about will give you no leverage in influencing his behavior. Observe your child and take note of what he expresses a liking for, what draws his interest, what he chooses and what he asks for. Though the item or privilege might seem small to you, it may matter enough to him to alter his behavior to keep it.

First Things First

One easy way of coming up with an appropriate Negative Consequence involves directly asking your child what he wants to do when he resists doing what you want. If you deem what he wants to do as safe and appropriate, simply inform him that in order to have the privilege of doing that, he *first* needs to do what you ask of him.

For instance, if your child refuses to get dressed in the morning, you might ask, "What would you rather do?"

She might respond, "I want to work on my puzzle."

"Well," you can then say, "In order to do that, you first have to be all dressed. And," you can add, "The sooner you do that, the more time you have to work on your puzzle."

The Promise Approach

In the same scenario, you can try The Promise Approach. You can say to your child, "Alright, you can work on your puzzle for five minutes, but then you must get dressed. Agreed?" You may be surprised at how often the child will fulfill his promise. If your child fails to live up to his end of the bargain, the next time he promises to do what you want after doing what he wants, you might say, "I would normally allow this, but the last time we made the agreement you did not stick to your end. Do it my way this time and we can try it again your way next time."

Within Your Power

It makes sense to select consequences that you have the power to impose without struggle. As you have learned, the moment you engage in a power struggle you incite more conflict. This is one reason why using the traditional time-out method with a child often proves so ineffective. If your child is already resisting doing what you want him to do, why would he suddenly willingly cooperate when you tell him to go to his room? We will discuss time-out in more detail soon. As parents, we need to be realistic enough to accept the limitations of our power of control, but make the best use of the power we have.

Using Conscious Detachment For Now

If your child runs out of the house to ride his bike, breaking your rule that he needs to clear the dinner table first, you may need to exercise Conscious Detachment *for now*, rather than yelling your head off or getting into a wrestling match over the doorknob to stop him from leaving. Don't worry that "he will think he won" if you fail to do something *immediately* to teach him that he cannot ignore your rules. Unless an immediate emergency exists, patiently and calmly work on bringing order into the situation by degrees.

You might, in this case, simply wait for him to come home. Say nothing about the situation upon his return, but openly express how much you love him and how glad you are that he came back safe and sound, even that you hope he enjoyed himself – and be sincere about all of this (based on the 95% Rule). If you express much frustration or disappointment over what happened, you may provide him with reverse encouragement by making him feel a sense of power over you. Then, later that night, while he is asleep, remove his bike to a secret location. When he notices that it is gone, explain to him that he has lost his bike privilege for a while for breaking the rule.

No Earning Back

I don't generally advocate requiring your child to earn back his privileges through special behavior. Simply impose a time limit on the privilege and when the time runs out, he gets another chance. Keep your time limits minimal, experimenting with briefer restraint periods first to see if they work.

Logical Connections

Base your choice of Negative Consequences on what you know your child likes. Trying to make every Negative Consequence into a perfectly logical result proves to be impossible and totally unnecessary. The Negative Consequence you impose needs no direct logical connection to the behavior you want because the system itself is inherently logical *when used appropriately.*

If your child breaks the rule that he makes his bed, for instance, you might impose a consequence of no TV for a day. The logical connection here lies in the fact that he has demonstrated irresponsibility relative to tidying and organizing his space. If an adult fails to adequately organize and tidy his space, the messy environment inevitably lowers his performance. This would negatively impact his earnings to the point that he would have to make some sacrifices, such as losing his cable connection for his TV. In other words, he would lose his TV viewing privilege.

Explain The Logic

The purpose of seeking your child's cooperation is *not* to make your child help you feel that you have superior power, to satisfy a desire you might have for an inflated sense of self-importance. The purpose is to support your child's ability to lead a responsible, quality life. By the time your child reaches his second plane of development, around the age of six, he will require an explanation of the logical purpose of your backing up rules with the restriction of privileges.

You might help him to understand, and thereby to cooperate, by saying something like, "Part of my job is to prepare you to live in the world on your own. In life, you have to fulfill certain responsibilities to preserve your privileges. By me linking your privileges to your responsible behavior now, I am preparing you to be able to do that for yourself later on. If I let you do as you please, you may lack the life-understanding and self-discipline to do what you need to do to take care of yourself when no one is there to support you."

Examples

Here are several examples of typical Consequences:
- "To watch your video, you need to first use the potty."
- "If you want to go to the mall with your friends, you need to wear something far less sexy."
- "If you want to play with your toy trucks next time, you have to put them away this time."
- "If you want to have a conversation with me, you need to speak with me respectfully."
- "If you want to go to the movies with your friends, you need to

be kind and considerate toward your stepdad."

- "If you want to ride your bike after dinner, you need to help clear the table first."

Gentle But Firm Physical Guidance

Using verbal warnings has little effect on children ages three and under. The most common form of privilege restriction to use is gentle, physical guidance, which is really a form of Building. In a firm but gentle manner, *physically prevent your child from doing what you want her not to do as you physically engage her in a safe, appropriate activity that she likes.*

About Time-Out

Basically, every form of Negative Consequence you employ represents a form of time-out. You may time a child out from the privilege of, say, riding his skateboard for a while if he rides it in a way that endangers others. To encourage him to follow the rule of putting his toys away, you can time your child out from playing with a particular toy for a while after he leaves it lying around. When a child behaves inappropriately in a particular environment, or toward a particular person, you can time the child out from that location or person.

Once you determine the Negative Consequence you will impose, the next logical question is, "How long?" How long should you time your child out from, say, playing with his truck, as a consequence for hitting his sister on the head with it? The length of time you choose comes down to a matter of your best judgment. Make the time of restriction last no longer than necessary. As has been said, it generally proves more constructive to err on the side of leniency before moving into firmer measures.

(UN)Timing Out To A Location

You may send or take the child to her room to end her inconsiderate behavior toward others, but do not require the child to spend any set amount of time away. I call this the "UNtimed-Out Method." As mild as this method may seem, it adequately establishes the boundary of acceptability, and it does so in a kind way that fosters and promotes the child's kindness and consideration.

When you use this method, be extremely sensitive to the child's feelings. You don't want to make the child see herself as an inferior, unworthy of love, respect, kindness or acceptance. Otherwise, you model the kind of insensitivity that you are striving to change. Your purpose is to teach your child to connect well with others and with her environment. Therefore, you must relate to her in a way that preserves the loving, respectful connection between you.

However soon the child chooses to leave her room and return to the location, start from scratch, as if nothing happened. Greet her warmly. Remember, your purpose is to lead her into behaving in a manner that demonstrates sensitive consideration for others. You need to demonstrate that with her consistently. If she resumes inconsiderate behavior, repeat the process. If, her behavior does not improve after two uses of this method, try implementing another consequence or use another Option.

If your child chooses to stay away, allow this as long as you can, but frequently check on her to make sure that she is feeling okay and behaving well where she is. When you check on her, express love and let her know that she does not have to stay where she is. If she is four or older, you can briefly mention the cause for your leading her there, but do not present a firm or angry demeanor, and then quickly let the matter go.

Exceptions And Locations

There are always exceptions, depending on the situation and the child's temperament at the time. Sometimes, for some children, you can direct him to remain in a time-out chair or room for a set time (no longer than one minute per year of life), But do this *only* if the child feels completely amenable to it. *If the child appears to feel the least bit saddened by an enforced amount of separation time, do not impose it.*

Choose locations in which you feel sure the child will feel safe and comfortable. Also be sure that she can physically reach you on her own without much effort when she wants to. If you are in someone else's home where your child does not feel absolutely comfortable and secure, do not use separation as a consequence.

Time-Out / Time-In

One form of separation consequence that may work nicely is a *Time-Out / Time-In*. You do this by joining your child in the separate location. While the separation helps her to develop a sense of considerate boundaries, your loving company nurtures her sense of caring connection. This tactic would not be a useful or appropriate response to her mistreating *you*.

You can use this method when your child behaves in an unruly manner in a public place. Have her sit next to you for a brief cooldown period without lecturing or chastising her. Remain loving. If she whines or demands to leave your side, warn that this will cause the time-out / time-in to last longer – or that you will leave the location with her for the day.

When To Use Separation

To improve a child's behavior, you may remove the child from a location or from a person as a consequence for behaving improperly in that location or toward that person. Don't send one child to his room, though, when he mistreats another, because that demeans the child, inciting more disturbing behavior.

Restaurants And Other Adult Locations

Don't use time-outs as a means of getting your child to behave well in a restaurant. The child who acts out in a particular restaurant is not yet ready for that type of restaurant. Leave that child home until he demonstrates enough self-control and understanding to handle that adult scene. In settings like church or temple, you may give the child a time-out / time-in for a break. From the age of five or six on, you can establish the rule that inappropriate behavior will earn the loss of a privilege later.

If The Child Won't Go

If your child refuses to go to a separate location on his own, you can carry him there if you have the physical strength to do so easily. After that point, though, do not engage in a wrestling match. Simply choose another Option, or another Negative Consequence, to bring about as much order to the situation as possible.

Timing Yourself Out

When you begin feeling frustrated or overwhelmed, *time yourself out*. Give yourself a cooling off break instead of struggling to force the child to give you a break. You can go into your room and close the door. If the child wants in, you can lock the door. As long as you feel confident that your child is safe on her own, give yourself the space you need.

If, for some reason, you cannot time yourself out when you need to, then concentrate on preserving your peace and poise no matter how out of control your child seems. Use Conscious Detachment for now. You don't really have any other sane choice.

Prearranged Consequences

For children around six-years of age and up, you can avoid arguments when you want cooperation by drawing up a list of the basic rules and responsibilities you expect your child to follow, and then a second list of the privileges your child enjoys. You then make it clear to your child that in order to receive the privileges on the first list, she needs to follow the rules and fulfill the responsibilities on the second list.

No Stickers, No Charts

Using a sticker system to reward and demerit your child into positive behavior confuses the child's values and hinders his natural motivation to behave well. By establishing a close, loving relationship with your child, surrounding your child with a stable, harmonious home-life, and applying your Child-Discipline Options correctly, you elicit from your child the very best she has to give.

Manipulation

Your clever child may attempt to turn your use of consequences against you by telling you that *you* have to do something for him in order for him to behave as you expect. Reverse this maneuver by letting him know what he will lose if he does not cooperate. For example you might say to your child, "I want you to get ready right now because we have to leave."

"If I do that, you have to buy me that new baseball glove," he might demand.

You might dispel this tactic by saying something like, "You want that new glove? We'll see. If you don't get ready right now, though, I guarantee there will be no new glove."

Another form of manipulation you might run into is the child's "I don't care" response. If your child seems not to care about the consequence, follow through anyway and see what happens. Sometimes the child says he doesn't care because he cares too much.

A child may also try to manipulate you by using the threat of an emotional blow up if you follow through. If your child does through a tantrum in response to receiving a consequence, calmly consider the possibility that you may be relating with him too harshly. If you decide that your rule ought to stand, compassionately apply the Option of Conscious Detachment while the tantrum ensues to teach him that this emotional manipulation tactic does not work.

After The Consequence

After you administer a consequence, go right into bonding with your child. For instance, when the child who attempted to bite you crawls back to you, *welcome her with open arms*. After you inform your child that she will not be permitted to watch TV because she did not complete her household chore, don't carry a grudge by remaining physically or emotionally removed. Giving your child a steady flow of love gives her the sense of security she needs to behave well.

The 1–2–3 Method

To be effective in your use of this Option, adhere to The No-Repeat Rule, which states that you are not to state a request, direction, or offer (see Building and Guiding Choices), more than two times in a row. After that, you either have to follow through on your Negative Consequence or choose another Option. If you repeat yourself more than that, you teach your child to habitually ignore your words. You also foster your own destructive habit of endlessly and pointlessly repeating yourself.

It is easier on both parent and child to warn a child about a Negative Consequence than to actually impose one on the child. If your child expects you to follow through, the vast majority of the time a warning or two is all that it will take for your child to change her behavior. That is one reason why I advocate as your standard operating procedure issuing a couple of warnings before following through on a Negative Consequence.

I do *not* advocate counting your warnings out loud, nor holding up your fingers to show your count, for your Negative Consequence Option. Count your warnings, requests, or directions to yourself. (You may, however, count out loud as a game that challenges the child to take action by the count of three. This would constitute a form of Building. If the child does not act before you reach three, stop the game and consider your other Options.)

Changing Your Mind

If your child tries to persuade you to change your mind by engaging in a responsible behavior *after* he has been informed that he has earned a consequence, sometimes it is okay for you to withdraw the Consequence. But you have to be careful here. If you do this too often you undermine the effectiveness of your warnings.

Sometimes, even if your child makes no effort to change your mind, after you think about it, you may come to the conclusion that you selected the wrong Option, that you should have, say, tried a Building approach or Conscious Detachment instead. There can be any number of reasons for changing your mind. Don't be so committed to consistency that you miss the opportunity to make things right in the present. If you realize later that an alternative approach would be the best for your child, change your mind.

You Do Not Need To Know The Consequence

By the time your child reaches six, you do not have to know what the Consequence will be even when you issue a warning. If you do not know what it will be, simply say, "If you do not do (or stop doing) that, you will receive a Negative Consequence." If he asks you what it will be, you might reply, "I don't know right now. But I will think about it and let you know if I am forced to follow through on it."

Consequences Without Warning

In some instances you might deem it more practical or appropriate to issue a Consequence without a warning. For instance, you might believe that your child has already received all the warnings necessary in the past. Perhaps what he did seems too serious for a warning. Sometimes, as in public settings, issuing a warning might trigger the child into even more disturbing behavior. In other instances, you may not be able to reach your child to inform her that she has overstepped her bounds or broken a rule. In still other instances, you might need time to think about what happened before deciding that imposing a Consequence without warnings would be your most effective response. In this case, you would inform him that he has a Negative Consequence and point out the behavior that necessitated it.

PART FIVE

PRIMARY PARENTING SOLUTIONS

Introduction
The Seven Pillars Of Child Discipline

There are no perfect solutions. Don't demand that you come up with a response to your child's behavior that will insure that she never behaves that way again and that proves flawless in every way. Sometimes the best you can do is to calmly direct her from a problematic behavior into a more appropriate behavior for the time being. When that is the best you can do in peace and poise, that *is* the best you can do.

The basic strategic guidelines that follow in this part of the book provide you with a framework on which to build your own unique, natural way of parenting with love in specific situations. However you choose to handle any particular parenting situation, think of your action as an experiment and seek to learn from the results. If something does not seem to be working, consider how you might alter your approach. Also consider the possibility that you are expecting too much change too quickly.

The Seven Pillars

The foundation of *every* solution that works for children and parents consists of what we may call *"The Seven Pillars Of Child Discipline"*:

1. Practice handling whatever happens with peace and poise.
2. Practice Conscious Parenting by paying close attention to what goes on between you and your child in every present moment.
3. From a foundation of conscious peace and poise, make it your first priority to create and sustain a positive connection with your child in which your child feels close to you and totally secure in your confidence, respect, deep love and appreciation.
4. Preserve the positive quality of your connection by adhering to

the 95% Rule: 95% of the time that you need to take action to keep your child's behavior on track, do so in a loving, pleasant, even playful way that she enjoys.

5. Provide your child with a stable, loving, harmonious home environment and a stable, orderly, unrushed daily routine.

6. Consistently model the behaviors and attitudes you want your child to display and eliminate, or at least minimize, any negative modeling to which she is exposed.

7. Be ready, willing and able to establish clear boundaries through the correct use (no anger) of Negative Consequences on those rare occasions (about 5% of the time) when Conscious Detachment or Building would be too passive or too mild in your estimation.

As you establish these "pillars," you provide your child with a *Parenting With Love Foundation* that supports his finest behaviors and attitudes, and insures that the challenges posed by his behavior will be easier for you to handle.

Solution 1:
Transitions

Two types of transition impact child behavior, The Transition From Activity And Place and The Transition Of Changing Circumstances. Children under the age of six (in the first plane of development), typically find both types most challenging, so what follows applies primarily, but not exclusively, to them.

The Transition From Activity And Place

The first type involves transitioning a child from one environment or activity into another. Ways to do this may include:

- Connect before you direct. First, focus on the child and bond with her in a loving, harmonious connection. Then issue your request or direction in harmony with her present feeling state.

- Listen to the tone of your voice. If you sound bossy or pushy, you incite your child's bossy "push-back." If you sound needy or pleading, the child perceives you as weak, annoying and out of control. An enthusiastic tone often works best.

- Avoid interrupting your first-plane child's focus of attention if you can at all help it. With this in mind, the ideal approach is to commence the leaving process before he begins a new project or task that you don't have time for him to complete. When you must interrupt, do so as gently and patiently as possible.

- If she ignores your verbal direction or request, rely on Building (95% of the time) by getting physically involved and using a pleasant, loving, even playful ways of leading the child into the next place or activity.

- As a last resort, you may try your Negative Consequence Option to motivate your child's cooperation; but for this or any other Option to work well, drop rush and tension from your mode.

The Transition of Changing Circumstances

The second type of transition that impacts child behavior occurs when disruption enters the child's life. The younger and more sensitive the child, and the more extreme the alteration of her circumstances, the more disturbed the child's behavior, thinking and emotions may be in response until normalcy settles back in.

The arrival of a new sibling, a change in a parent's schedule, moving to a new home or neighborhood, even shifting the furniture around can produce some degree of regression including a reversion to pre-potty training, stepped up displays of disrespectfulness or aggressiveness, a lack of focus at school or a hair-trigger tantrum pattern. Ways to counteract the regressive behavior include:

- Regard regression as a normal, natural, temporary response to transition. All of us feel somewhat challenged by the sense of uncertainty and loss of control that comes with change. If *you* feel emotionally challenged by a change, concentrate on regaining your balance as your first priority.

- Rely on Conscious Detachment to cut your child (and yourself) some extra slack during the testy period of adjustment.

- Restore the order to your child's schedules and surroundings as soon as possible.

- Because of the added stress of change, rely on your Building Option more than ever when you need to take action.

- When you need to resort to your Negative Consequence Option, express more compassion, understanding and patience in light of your child's (and possibly your own) difficult adjustment period.

Solution 2
Bedtime (Including Nighttime-Crying, Bed-Leaving, Naptime)

Children are most sensitive and suggestible at the close of the day. The attitude you express toward and around them at this time sinks in to influence them most deeply. Therefore, however your child behaves at this time, remain kind, at peace, and aware of the child's feelings.

If your child has difficulty going to sleep, consider the possibility that he has been exposed to too much stressful intensity or emotionally upsetting experiences during the day. Providing your child with a stable, orderly, unhurried, harmonious daily routine provides a necessary foundation for a peaceful night. Make improvements to your child's overall situation as needed to support your bedtime strategy.

Understand also that all human beings awaken in the night. When young children do so, they often instinctively count on the person who put them to bed to send them off to sleep again. A child's nighttime sleep interruption pattern can go on for years. By remaining as calm as possible when it occurs, you maximize your rest. In other words, you may simply have to learn how to adapt to this one.

What follows primarily applies to parents who choose to have their child spend the night in the child's own bed and not in the parent's bed. Repeat these procedures consistently until your child realizes that the bedtime structure is basically inflexible.

At bedtime, place your infant in her crib *before* she falls asleep. Otherwise, you teach her to need to feel your arms around her in order to fall asleep.

Beginning about the age of two, give her a low-lying bed that she can leave and enter at will. The crib that used to protect her now feels confining and causes a sense of separation that makes her more emotionally unsettled and dependent.

Consider the following solutions:

- Begin bedtime preparations one hour before you expect your child to be in bed with the lights out.
- Keep the environment quiet, peaceful and harmonious as bedtime approaches.
- If your young child likes to run around and play hard right before bedtime, allow and even encourage that. It wears him out.
- During bedtime preparations, keep your voice tones soft and your manner mild.
- You might plant the seed in your child's mind about the approach of bedtime. Beginning fifteen minutes before bedtime, *gently* remind him every five minutes of bedtime's approach (unless this upsets him and incites his resistance).
- Establish a bedtime ritual. The more regularity you bring into your child's bedtime procedure, the more smoothly it will flow.
- Leave her room the same time every night, or as close to that as possible.
- If your child cries when you leave, listen to the sound before responding. She may need to cry to relieve herself of her last bit of tension before falling soundly asleep. Definitely do *not* react with frustration, yelling, pleading, criticizing or complaining.
- If her cries sound tragic or urgent, check on her. Address any real needs she may have and provide her with a few moments of loving soothing.
- If your child makes special requests, like wanting a drink of water, do not cooperate with this endlessly. Calmly and compassionately, yet firmly, draw the line after fulfilling one or two requests.
- You may gently introduce your Negative Consequence Option to motivate cooperation. For instance, you might warn your child of the loss of a privilege the following day (for children around five and older), or that you will leave his room at the usual time even if it means no story time.

If Your Child Leaves Bed

If your child leaves her bed and wanders out of her room after bedtime, remain totally calm. Your becoming stressed would only add to his restlessness and antagonize him. Maintain an atmosphere of peace and quiet. Do *not* treat this behavior as a big deal by turning it into a major conflict. Establish yourself in a patient, trusting, peaceful attitude.

Ask her to return to her room. If she resists, offer to go there with her. Do not complain or criticize on the way. Remain calm and as quiet as possible.

If she refuses to go back to her room within a few moments, practice Conscious Detachment. Make the environment quiet. Turn off the TV and dim the lights. Do not play with her or engage in conversation. You want to make the environment as uninteresting for her as possible.

If she continues to refuse to return to her room, you can carry her there as a last resort (if she is light enough) even if she cries. She may then cry herself to sleep. For children four years of age and older, you can warn of a Negative Consequence to be administered the following day.

Note: However, it may work best to experiment with a more lenient approach first. Let her experience the freedom to be out of bed for a while, letting her see that there is really nothing special to be gained from this. It also may work, as a Building approach, to let her lie down on the couch beside you and fall asleep there. Don't let this turn into a routine, but as an exception it can provide her with essential bonding that builds deep emotional security.

For children who wander out in the first three years, consider the use of a baby gate. The first time that your child wanders out, warn him that you will lock the baby gate in his doorway if he does not remain in his room. Repeat your warning the second time he leaves. If it happens a third time, follow through and lock the baby gate.

Note: Definitely do *not* warn or follow through by closing the child's bedroom door, or locking it to keep him in. The baby-gate allows the child to see out and feel connected to you and to the rest of the home, which she needs in order to feel safe and cared for. *You should still go to him if he cries, following the night-crying procedure described above.* If your child climbs over the gate or knocks it down, he has outgrown the usefulness of this procedure.

Wants To Join You In Your Bed

If he comes into your room while you are in bed in the night, gently but firmly and consistently send him back to his room.

If he refuses to return to his room on his own, calmly and kindly escort him, engaging in as little talking as possible, because talking stimulates the child. If he speaks to you, respond in a whisper. Be consistent, repeating this procedure as many times and as many nights as necessary.

Exceptions To The Rule: If your child is sick, frightened by a storm, or unsettled by some other special disturbance or transition, the kind thing to do may be to allow her to sleep in your bed or for you to remain with her longer than usual in her bed. Return to the stable routine as soon as possible and don't be surprised if it takes a while to re-adapt him to his standard routine.

In the very early morning, if your young child comes to you at dawn with a desire to sleep the final hour or two with you, allow that. This close snuggle time nurtures the child and fosters a deep emotional connection that supports him (and maybe sustains you in an important way) for the rest of the day.

Teenaged children may want to remain up after *your* bedtime. Enforce the rule of no TV, telephone or computer use after *your* bedtime, and allow reading only that which you approve of. If your child breaks this rule, employ your Negative Consequence Option.

Nap Time

Children generally do best when they nap on a daily basis through the age of four. (Adults do best with a daily nap lasting about 15 to 30 minutes.)

Try to have your child nap in the same place, at the same time, each day. When he begins outgrowing his nap, try to have him stay in quiet time for the same period of time each day.

Don't try to enforce a nap with stress and strain. You need to be relaxed for your child to relax. Rely on Building. If your child refuses to nap, definitely don't squabble about it and don't institute Negative Consequences. Try to provide him with some low-key time if possible, and find creative ways to get done what you hoped to accomplish while he napped.

Solution 3:
Up And Out In The Morning

Think of morning as the day's springboard: what occurs at the start of the day sets the tone for the remainder of the day. When you feel pressured to get your child moving, you interact with her in a mode of struggle and strain, anger and impatience. This sends her on a course of lower performance for that day. A harmonious, loving morning experience prepares your child for a happy, success-filled day.

- Establish a set weekday morning routine and stick to it consistently.
- For children under six, a period of bonding, in which the child establishes a secure connection with home and with you should precede launching him into the day. Provide at least 30 minutes of your undivided, loving attention and involvement before he has to get ready to leave.
- The child-discipline problem you think you have in the morning may actually be your own time-management problem. If your child's slow pace causes you stress, re-design your morning schedule. You may have to go to bed earlier yourself to wake up earlier so you have the time to bond and lead your child through the stages of morning preparation in a calm, unstrained manner.
- Gradually turn more and more of your child's morning tasks over to him. However, don't be too firm here. Your involvement in preparations may provide needed bonding.
- If your child appears to dawdle, rely on Building to accelerate your child's preparations. For instance, create a game of getting dressed.
- If your child is running late and has no time to eat, offer food-on-the-run (like a nutritious breakfast bar). Later, look back at what brought this about so you can avoid it in the future.

- If your child refuses to eat, honor her natural appetite. (Stressfully struggling to make a child eat can only shut down her appetite, anyway.) If she feels very hungry later, she will learn from the Natural Consequence to better manage her food intake.
- If your child refuses to get ready, preferring to watch TV or engage in some other activity that she likes, use your Negative Consequence Option by informing her that you will no longer allow that privilege in the morning if she does not get ready right now. (You can then reinstate the privilege a day or so later if she still wants it, as long as she agrees to cooperate with the morning routine. Then see how that goes.)
- If your child under six does not wake up punctually on his own, awaken him gently or save time by dressing him in his sleep first (which may gently awaken him). If he consistently oversleeps, make his bedtime earlier.
- If your child over the age of six does not wake up on time, wake him. If that becomes burdensome for you, give him an alarm clock and explain that his waking up and leaving on time is his responsibility, not yours. Therefore, you will give him no more than two chances. If he ignores the alarm and oversleeps a third time, he will lose a privilege (see your Negative Consequence Option). Follow through if that becomes necessary.

Solution 4:
Whining

The fact is that children inevitably whine at times. Adults also whine. (If you don't think that *you* whine, listen to yourself more closely.) Based on The Law Of Reflection, the more you whine around or at your child, the more you *make* your child whine. Based on The Law Of Results, if your child's whining makes you react with anger or stress, you teach her to whine for control.

- Treat whining as a natural, little annoyance, like mosquitoes in summer. The more calmly you handle it, the less of a toll it will take, and the less your child will use it to control you.
- A child often begins whining when her parent ignores her normal tone. Practice being more aware of and responsive to the sound of your child's normal voice. When your child speaks to you, stop what you are doing and give your child undivided attention. Listen to what she wants and provide her with a clear, direct response.
- When she whines, use The Law Of Reflection. Rather than asking or telling your child to stop whining, say something like, "Here is how to ask me for that..." and then demonstrate exactly how you want her to sound. When she asks properly, give her your response.
- If she continues whining because she does not like your response, try using Conscious Detachment (for a good five minutes if necessary) to remove her incentive from using that tactic for attention or control.
- If that does not work soon enough for you, of if you would prefer a more assertive approach, use your Building Option 95% of the time. For instance, you might start singing a song she

likes to distract her, or begin chasing her around playfully. Don't worry that this will reward her behavior. It builds bonding that supports her desire to demonstrate her finest behavior.

- If the whining continues, or your best judgment (from peace and poise) advises that you take a firmer stand at this time, resort to your Guiding Choices Options by offering her two choices, both of which you find acceptable. For instance, if she whines for ice cream for breakfast, you can offer her the choice of hot cereal or cinnamon toast.

- If Guiding Choices does not do the trick and you want to take firmer action, move onto your Negative Consequence Option. You might warn, "If you continue asking me for ice cream, there will be no ice cream at all for the whole day." However, if the child is too emotionally worked up, this may not stop the whining and you will then need to return to Conscious Detachment anyway.

- An UNtimed Out can be used as your Negative Consequence for whining. Here, you send or escort her to her room and then leave, allowing her to leave the room when she wants. This teaches the child that whining oversteps the boundaries of respect. When she returns to you, be loving and welcoming and avoid referring to the whining at all. If she reverts to whining, you can repeat this procedure. If this continues happening, it will likely turn into a game, which is okay. Then, you would both be having a pleasant time together and the whining will have ended. This serves your purpose because the less your child indulges in whining, the less of a habit whining becomes for her.

Solution 5:
Displays Of "Disrespect"

From time to time your child will speak to you in a bossy, disrespectful tone or pay no attention to you in a way that causes you to feel disrespected. To handle this effectively, realize that how you *interpret* your child's behavior causes your emotional reaction to that behavior. That is why I place the term "Disrespect" in quotation marks in the title. When you feel disrespected, regard how you feel as your way of interpreting what occurred and then reacting to your interpretation.

Beyond this, based on The Law Of Reflection, you teach a child to express a bossy, disrespectful attitude when you expose him to a bossy, disrespectful model. The more harsh criticism, condescension, bossiness, pushiness, or hostility you demonstrate around the child, the more the child learns to demonstrate those qualities.

Based on The Law Of Results, if your child can make you react with anger or stress by expressing a disrespectful attitude, your reaction may give him the sense of power and control that he is after, thus reinforcing that behavior.

Bear in mind also that all human beings speak and act more crudely when we feel annoyed, tired or upset. This does not mean that you ought to condone or to encourage disrespectful conduct. Just understand that, while you can minimize it by applying some sensible procedures, you need to tolerate some of it with compassionate understanding.

When your child expresses rudeness, take it as a sign that you need to pay closer attention to the qualities exhibited by yourself and by others in his surroundings. Improve your child's surrounding influences to improve your child's attitude.

Parents of children under six commonly regard the child as

being disrespectful when the child appears to ignore the parent's efforts to get his attention. As you read in the section on Planes Of Development, children under six are in the process of developing their power to concentrate. Distracting the child from his concentration serves to weaken the child's control over his attention, making him more distractible. Additionally, the child during these years does not yet have the power to control his attention "at will." So, rather than interpreting his seeming to ignore you as disrespectful, improve the timing of your attempt to draw his attention.

As was stated in the solution on whining, children often speak disrespectfully when the polite way of speaking is ignored. Practice being more alert to recognize and respond when your child speaks respectfully.

When your child speaks in a disrespectful manner, let him know how you want him to speak by saying something like, "This is how I want you to say that." Then ask him to restate what he has to say in that respectful way.

If he continues speaking in a rude fashion, let him know that you will not engage in conversation until he speaks respectfully. Use Conscious Detachment for a while if his manner doesn't improve. After that, you can resort to your Negative Consequence Option by warning him of the loss of privilege that will follow if he does not improve his manner of speaking. Be sure to speak calmly, clearly, and in a dignified manner as you state this, to continue your positive modeling.

If he is making a rude demand for something you are willing to do for him, you can make your compliance with the demand contingent on his making the request in a respectful manner.

Meeting And Greeting

Explain and demonstrate the proper forms of meeting and greeting, and relating in general.

A child who feels shy or sensitive may appear disrespectful without intending to do so. Allow the child to establish her own sense of comfortable boundaries as you consistently demonstrate considerate, respectful, polite social skills in her presence.

A shy child often reflects shyness felt by the parent. At the same time, to compensate for her own shyness, a parent may try to force her child to be more outgoing. As you honestly address and deal with your own shyness, your child may handle her own sensitivity more adeptly.

For children ages six and older, make polite greeting and interacting a rule that you back up with your Negative Consequence Option. However, before resorting to this option, have a conversation aimed at discovering any reasons for the rude behavior. She may have a good one. For instance, the person she withdraws from may have mistreated her or may remind of someone who has, and she needs your help in handling this challenging situation properly.

Solution 6:
Tantrums

From time to time, every healthy child tantrums, if for no other reason than as a form of stress reduction. In other words, an occasional tantrum cannot be avoided and should be regarded as a healthy release of pent-up frustration or unhappiness.

When your child throws a tantrum, consider first that a legitimate need of the child is being overlooked or that a need is so routinely ignored that the child automatically shifts into panic-mode in response to slight dissatisfaction. Pay closer attention to how you and others relate with your child, and to your child's surroundings, to discover any ways that the child's needs are not being met. For instance, a sensitive child may tantrum when her surroundings are simply too intense, or the people around her behave too aggressively, making her feel unsettled, insecure and out of control.

That being said, when a child routinely melts down (or blows up) emotionally, that reaction ingrains itself as her habitual response to not instantly getting her way. Therefore, you want to do everything possible to avoid *needlessly* causing or contributing to a child's tantrums.

- If your child over the age of one year tantrums even once a day, consider the possibility that you, or someone else, drives her into a tantrum by needlessly and excessively restricting her freedom of movement and activity. In other words, her tantrum pattern expresses a legitimate need.
- Instead of automatically blocking your child from doing what he wants, as much as is feasibly possible seek a way to help her to satisfy her needs in a safe, responsible manner. For instance, if she wants to touch something breakable, help her to touch it safely by keeping your hands close and ready to intervene when

necessary. Parents often intervene too quickly because they *expect* a problem, when giving the child a bit more freedom and responsibility would have worked out fine.

- To avoid needlessly triggering your child's tantrum, pay close attention to him during your interactions. As soon as you see signs of his resistance or opposition, stop, step back, and consider your options for a more flexible approach or compromise rather than blindly forging on.

- Based on The Law Of Reflection, exposing a child to too much intensity, aggression or rage drives the child into emotional maelstroms.

- A child routinely tantrums when the tantrums cause the parents to give the child what he tantrums for (encouraging the tantrum based on The Law Of Results).

    Note: *If your child tantrums for a good reason, expressing a legitimate need, definitely do not withhold what the child cries for in an effort to avoid teaching her not to tantrum.*

- Children tantrum routinely when those people the child counts on routinely overlook the child's healthier, more appropriate forms of self-expression. Pay close attention to your child to alertly recognize and respond to her way of communicating *before* she feels compelled to blow up to make her point.

- When your child throws a tantrum, do not attempt to reason or talk her out of it. If her tantrum is real, reason and words won't reach her. If she is using it to manipulate you, your efforts to calm her down may convey the message that she has gained control over you through her emotional tactic. Give her some freedom to vent her feelings.

- The more emotionally worked up your child, the more established in peace and poise you need to be, because your feelings radiate and influence your child to feel similarly. If you allow your child's tantrum to trigger you into an emotional reaction, you add fuel to the fire.

- If the tantrum takes place in a public place, and calm Conscious Detachment does not work quickly, remove your child from that location to avoid her developing the habit of tantruming in public and to avoid teaching her that it is acceptable to do so.

- For children five years and older, engage in a discussion at a later time, in a private location, in which you briefly and simply explain that being overbearing and emotional in public demonstrates disrespect toward others. Then warn that he will receive a Negative Consequence involving the restriction of some privilege if it happens again.

- If the tantrum takes place at home, try simply walking away to teach him that he cannot control you with tantrums, and that you will show yourself enough respect to place some space between you and the commotion.

- Stay away until the intensity of the outburst subsides, or unless the sound of the cries expresses a genuine need for your assistance.

- If he follows you, go to *your* room (and hold the door shut if he tries to get in, as long as the child is safe on his own).

- If he begs you to come to him or to let him in, state in a calm voice that he needs to quiet down first. If he is crying too loudly to hear you, do not raise your voice to be heard, as your becoming loud will provoke him to stay loud.

- If you cannot separate yourself for some reason, you have no sane alternative but to withstand the outburst with peace and poise for as long as it lasts. For children five years and older who can understand consequences imposed after the fact, you can inform him later that forcing you to bear his tantrum without giving you space has earned him a Negative Consequence.

    Note: *It generally proves counter productive to demand that a child go to his room (or to some other cooling off location) when he tantrums, **unless he quickly and easily cooperates with that direction**. With a child small enough for you, you can carry her to her room for an UNtimed out (see how this works in the chapter explaining your Negative Consequence Option) to demonstrate that an emotional tirade in close proximity of others oversteps the boundaries of respectful consideration of them.*

Solution 7:
Physical Aggression
(Biting, Hitting, Running Into The Street, Etc.)

When a child demonstrates excessive physical aggression toward anyone or anything, the last thing that child needs is exposure to *your* aggression. Based on The Law of Reflection, demonstrating physical aggression toward or around a child leads the child into physical aggression.

Be aware that children sometimes try to bite when they feel hungry or when teething. Sometimes a child uses physical aggression when he wants a more physically assertive form of loving.

If your child bites, offer him something to eat. If that does not work, offer him something to chew upon. If that doesn't work, or if he engages in some other form of physical aggression with you, engage in some affectionate roughhousing with her for a while.

Don't worry that this will teach her to use physical aggression inappropriately. It provides a deep, close form of bonding that nurtures the child's heart and fosters her finest behavior.

When your better judgment suggests a firm establishment of appropriate boundaries, consider the following.

When A Child Is Physically Aggressive Toward You

To eliminate the influences that would cause or contribute to your child's excessive aggressiveness, the first place to look is at the quality of influences impacting your child. Children who routinely spend time in chaotic and intense settings, or who witness violent, destructive behavior (even on TV) are most likely going to demonstrate a pattern of overly aggressive behavior themselves.

- Using any form of corporeal punishment *for any reason* encourages a child's use of physically aggressive behavior including biting, hitting, kicking, spitting, breaking things intentionally, and shoving others around.

- Exposing a child under the age of six to much emotional, verbal aggression, impatience and rush triggers the child's physical aggression.

- Use no expressions of anger to discourage physical aggression because an angry reaction to *any* behavior provokes the child to repeat that behavior even more aggressively.

- Based on The Law Of Repetition, any behavior a child engages in repeatedly grows into a habit. Therefore, use a preemptive strategy rather than a reactive strategy. This requires that you pay close enough attention to see the act of physical aggression coming.

- When you see it coming, clearly state, "Hitting (or whatever form of attack he is using) is not allowed." Then, physically prevent the child from committing the act. You can prevent a bite by holding your hand against the child's forehead as he attempts to move his teeth toward you. You can hold your child's hand or foot if he attempts to strike you with one of those.

    Note: *Definitely do **not** hold the child in a way that causes the child pain, as this not only can hurt the child, but it incites even more physical aggression. Also, do not continue to physically restrain the child (for this would amount to a form of corporeal punishment). Release her as soon as possible.*

- If she tries to attack again, repeat the above preventative procedure. Then, place some space between you and the child (but not so much space that she cannot easily reach you). When the child returns, welcome her and act as if nothing has happened. If she repeats the attempt to attack, repeat your procedure.

- If the child is older than three years, you can warn of a Negative Consequence if the aggressive behavior continues. For instance, you can say something like, "If you continue to try to hit me, I will take your favorite truck and put it away for a while."

- If he is older than three, and is hitting you because he wants you to do something, you can say, "If you want me to... (what he wants you to do) here is how to ask me." Then state it just the way you want to hear it. You can also use your Negative Consequence Option by saying something like, "If you continue to kick me, I definitely will not... (do what he wants you to do)."

- If the act of aggression has already occurred, remain calm. State that hitting (biting, kicking, or whatever form of physical aggression she used) is not allowed. For children under age six, place some space between you and the child, following the guidelines in solution 6. For children six and older, you can warn of a Negative Consequence or issue one without warning. For instance, you might say, "Because you hit me, here is what you lose."

When A Child Is Physically Aggressive Toward Another

When a child becomes physically aggressive toward another child by, say, snatching toys away, shoving, hitting, spitting, etc. or in any way physically mistreats a pet, *immediately intervene.*

If a clear, firm verbal direction does not prove adequate, step in *calmly and confidently, with absolutely no show of anger,* by physically separating the aggressor from the one attacked.

Next, go to the one who received the rough treatment and provide loving care. Permit the aggressor to observe this.

Then go over to the aggressor and correct in a way that demonstrates loving kindness. (Remember that loving-kindness is not a reward, but a necessity, and by you demonstrating it when you feel like reacting harshly, you lead the child by example to exercise a higher level of self-control.) In a loving (not pleading) manner, say to the child something like, "I love you and I want you to treat others in a loving way. It is not okay for us to hurt anyone, not even to hurt their feelings." Then provide that child with some gentle phys-ical affection to model loving care expressed physically. For children with sufficient verbal ability (usually no younger than four), you can try asking what happened and then suggest a better way for him to handle that in the future.

If the aggressive pattern persists, you need to pay closer atten-tion to the aggressive child and position yourself physically to pre-vent further physical assault before it happens.

For children four years of age and older, you can introduce your Negative Consequence Option to discourage mistreatment of oth-ers. For instance, you might warn, "If you continue to block Andrew's way like that, you will not be permitted to play on the playground for a while."

If you have a child who routinely shows aggression, observe her to find out what situations provoke her. For children under six, pro-vide a demonstration of how to properly handle such situations. For children over six, you can discuss the situations and together come up with an acceptable strategy for dealing with those sorts of situa-tions.

If the child's aggressive treatment of another continues, you have no choice but to temporarily physically separate that child from the person or pet he seems committed to mistreating.

If the child's aggressive treatment continues, regard that as a sign that something is troubling her. She may need to kick a pillow around. There may be something going on in her life that you need to do something about.

Mistreating Objects

When a child handles an object too aggressively or destructive-ly, try using Building by giving him something appropriate to treat that way. For instance, if he wants to bash a toy truck upon the floor, give him a pillow to bash against the floor, or take him out-side and let him slam sticks against a rock or tree.

If the child insists on mistreating a particular object, the Negative Consequence can be your removal of the object for a while, even if he cries about it.

Running Into The Street

When a child runs into the street or launches into some other form of dangerous activity, base your response on the child's age. For children under the age of six, take all the responsibility for keeping your child safe. You need to pay close enough attention and *be in physically close enough proximity to the child* to physically prevent him from injury. Reacting after the fact may be too late.

Do not use spanking to "teach" a child to demonstrate more care and respect for his body! Any form of corporeal punishment models *disrespect* for physical boundaries and fails to insure the child's future self-control. Treat the child's body and feelings with the utmost respect, for that teaches the child to take the very best possible care of herself.

Solution 8:
Mealtime Behavior

Children typically demonstrate eating patterns similar to the eating patterns displayed around them. However, a sensitive child may demonstrate more limited tastes in food, particularly in the context of a stressful household. Additionally, when parents use force in an attempt to "make" a child eat, their efforts produce a backlash effect, driving the child to oppose his own natural inclinations in an act of will.

Mealtime presents a special opportunity for sacred nurturing of the family's physical *and* spiritual unity. Do your best to have at least dinner together every day, and follow the same basic routine and rituals on a regular basis. This brings a sense of stability and security into your child's life that supports the child's orderly, harmonious behavior and positive self-motivation.

A common mistake parents make at mealtime involves "force feeding" the child on education in manners. Regard nothing as more important for the child than to experience loving, harmonious bonding around the table. As the child matures, he naturally picks up the level of well-mannered politeness you consistently demonstrate. When you attempt to "force feed" lessons in manners, you treat your child as more in need of your control then he actually is, provoke a meal of contention and strife, and instigate the child's rebellious disdain for politeness.

A harmonious mealtime that everyone fully enjoys will do the child more good than stern attitudes of correction and complaint. Trust that as your child matures he will develop the capacity to understand and appreciate table etiquette (by the age of five) and have the happiness in his heart to want to demonstrate it.

This being said, however, you can do certain things to promote good manners and establish some basic boundaries that help the child receive a clear message about the rules of polite table conduct.

- Demonstrate the level of politeness you expect from your child, but don't value a polite exterior over a genuine spirit of heartfelt kindness and love. Otherwise, you "feed" your child on false values.

- Remain peaceful and harmonious during the meal you share together. If the child gets worked up, keep *yourself* settled down. Deal with what happens calmly, compassionately, patiently and confidently.

- If the child behaves in a manner that disturbs you or other individuals at the table, calmly and compassionately remove him from the table out of respect for the others. But as you do this, remain sensitively considerate of the child's feelings as well, otherwise you give him a mixed message about respecting others. Do not humiliate or embarrass the child. Let the child return to the table when she chooses and start from scratch, as if nothing happened. Repeat this procedure as often as needed. Do not coax the child to return to the table if she gets engaged in something else. Let everyone enjoy the meal in peace and harmony.

- Dinnertime offers an excellent opportunity for the family to digest the day's experiences, as every experience one has impacts every other family member. Do not bring up heavy issues, though, and keep your voice tones soft and sweet. Refuse to engage in intense conversation at the table and carefully avoid bringing up disturbing topics of conversation. Engage in no petty gossip, criticism, or complaining regarding any person or situation.

- Eat consciously and without haste.

- Don't expect to concentrate on a discussion with your mate or a guest at the exclusion of your young child. Share attention equally among all who are present and give everyone equal time for self-expression. However, to keep a young child on track, you may need to remain very involved with her, meaning you will have less time to share with others.

- When you feel the need to correct or to direct your child, do so most sensitively and compassionately. Stress at mealtime sickens the body and the soul of everyone present.

- During the first three years of life, encourage your child to remain seated at the table and help him to do so by giving him plenty of calm, patient, loving attention and involvement while he is at the table. It may help to give your child some intense activity beforehand so that settling at the table will be easier for him.

- Don't go into "automatic critic mode." If your child shows poor manners, he may be using it for attention. You might try using Conscious Detachment as your response. Then, when he behaves well, give him attention (your Building Option).

- If you want to try a more formal approach, calmly and kindly say something like: "This is the well-mannered way." Then demonstrate that way. If necessary, repeat this three times. However, gauge the effects of this. If it produces the opposite of the results you are after, change your approach for better results.

- If you want to try a more assertive approach, you might say, "If you continue to ("spit out your food," "bang your fork on the table," or whatever other behavior you want to discourage) you will need to leave the table." If he chooses that option, let that occur. Your top priority is to preserve the peaceful harmony at the table.

- It is normal for children under eighteen months to spit out food when they feel full or do not like the taste. Also, they may spit out the food as a natural part of their exploration of the food or to exercise their mouth. Calmly provide the child with a napkin to spit in more politely. You can minimize food-spitting by giving tiny tastes of food you offer the child to try.

- If your child under six throws food, take that as a sign that you need to be more engaged with her before she throws. When you see her about to throw, do not simply use words to prevent it. Gently but firmly take hold of her hand and remove the food before she throws it. If she cries, remain calm. You might give her something else to throw, like a napkin. If the crying continues, calmly remove her from the table and follow the UNtimed out routine you learned in the chapter on Negative Consequences.

- Children sometimes throw food when they are ready to be done with the meal. If that is the case, let the child leave the table and you go back to enjoying the meal.

- Don't force a child to remain seated at the table until everyone is through. It is healthier for him to move about during his digestion period than to remain seated, just as it is healthy for you to take a walk after a meal.

- If your child under three has difficulty staying in his seat during the meal or would prefer to take bites and then go off and work with his toy trucks, then return for more bites, permit this. Let him engage in all the work he wants, because the more he works the more he develops. As he matures and you make mealtime a peaceful time of family harmony, he will want to remain at the table for longer periods.

- If your child shows little interest in food, it may be that there is too much stress in the household. Or, it may simply be that he is one of those people (like you, perhaps?) who shows more interest in activity than in food. You will find that very healthy and fit people often show little interest in eating.

- Children typically eat like birds for days, and then gorge like a horse for a day or so. Make no effort to force a child to taste what he does not want, and make no effort to force your child to eat more when he says that he feels full. You want your child to follow her natural, healthy appetite sensations. If you teach her to ignore these, you prepare the child for over-eating that may result in obesity. A child exhibits better discrimination as to what to eat, rejecting junk food and choosing healthy foods,

when you honor the child's natural inclinations. If she leaves
food on her plate, give her – or have her give herself – smaller
portions. In any event, it is better to waste the food in the trash
than to force it into a full stomach.

- If your child eats very little or nothing for dinner, and then say's
she is hungry later in the evening, offer her something simple to
eat. This is to honor your child's natural appetite pattern. This
proves healthier than forcing a child to develop a habit of eating when she is not truly hungry.

- To encourage eating healthy foods, do not make junk foods
available, and do not indulge in junk food yourself. When a
child wants junk food, don't immediately oppose this idea.
Sometimes letting him have a taste makes him realize that he
really does not want that after all. Don't automatically presume
that your child needs your guidance and control. Stepping in
and excessively controlling dulls the child's sense of his own
intelligent, internal guidance system.

- If, for whatever reason, she shows poor judgment and would fill
up on junk food instead of good food, simply refuse that. If she
uses a negative control tactic, like shouting a demand at you,
remain calm and say something like, "If you continue demanding...("ice cream" or "a cookie" or whatever she is demanding)
for dinner, there will be no...(whatever she is demanding)
for...(decide on a period of time)."

- When your child wants something from the kitchen after everyone is seated at the table, do not automatically get it for her.
Either she gets it for herself or she joins you in getting it. This
teaches her respectful table manners and fosters self-reliance.
Here again, though, don't be a stickler at the table or you ruin
the peaceful atmosphere. Be harmoniously flexible.

- If your child does not want to eat what you prepare, consider
her tastes before preparing meals. Serve your child a meal you
know that she likes rather than hoping she will like something

new. You don't have to eat what your child eats and your child does not have to eat what you eat.

- If she rejects the meal that has been prepared, give her one more option, something quick and simple, like a sandwich. If that does not appeal to her, presume she's just not hungry. Keep in mind, however, that children tend to show more interest in a meal that they have participated in preparing and serving.
- From the age of eighteen months, routinely involve your child in at least some of the activities of meal preparation, meal service and meal clean up. Children at this stage tend to show more interest in their food when they take part in the work that goes into the meal. Additionally, it instills competence and self-reliance.

Special Dietary Needs and Medication

If your child has special dietary requirements and resists complying with them, remain calm and consider your Child-Direction Options. *Only* if necessity demands it, resort to force-feeding your child, compassionately and unemotionally. By the time your child reaches the age of six, you can help him to understand his special needs and the dire consequences of not meeting them. If your child continues to resist doing what is good for her, take a close look at the factors impacting her behavior covered throughout this book and make adjustments where needed. (Also, look at the following solution 9: Hygiene.)

Solution 9: Hygiene

Children under the age of six resist hand washing, bathing, and teeth brushing out of a natural and healthy sense of ownership over their own body *because they do not fully comprehend the importance of hygiene.* Children older than six do this *because they don't care enough about themselves.*

If you react to your child with much frustration or disapproval, you instigate stiffer resistance and rebellion and run the risk of damaging your relationship with your child. This works against you (and your child) because it lowers the child's self-esteem, *and poor hygiene is a symptom of low self-esteem.*

An unclean body and slovenly appearance represent ways that a child expresses feelings of unworthiness, guilt, unhappiness and shame. If your child demonstrates poor hygiene, or a resistance to taking the actions necessary for cleanliness, adhere to the general guidelines you have been learning throughout this book, with particular consideration of the following.

- Based on The Law Of Reflection, how much you will have to work at your child's cooperation in the area of hygiene may depend, in part, upon how willful, independent and unruly are the people around your child. Also based on this Law, a child's resistance to hygiene may indicate that a person around your child suffers from low self-esteem and expresses it through poor hygiene.
- Parents mildly panic when a child refuses to, say, wash his hands after playing outside. However, when you feel anxious while attempting to direct your child, your anxiety translates into nervous, overly stern or harsh aggressiveness that intensifies the

child's defensiveness and opposition. Obviously, you cannot permit your child to remain unclean indefinitely but do not let this thought drive you to pursue your child's cleanliness too aggressively.

- As important as hygiene is, and as much as you *don't* want to spend a lot of your time gaining your child's cooperation, you will achieve the best results here, as in all other situations, by maintaining your composure, your confidence, and your patience while remaining committed to your achieving your objective.

- To more easily direct, first connect. Your child needs to feel that *she* counts to you more than her behavior does. Therefore, if you run into much resistance regarding hygiene, take that as a sign that you may need to work on developing a more loving, harmonious way of relating with your child in general.

- Keep hygiene in perspective. For your child to be healthy, she also needs a harmonious home-life and a happy, loving relationship with you. These serve as the foundation for the child wanting to make the best choices for herself. Thus, on occasion, you might have to skip a hand or face wash or teeth brushing for the healthful benefits of peace and harmony.

- Explain the importance of hygiene to your child, beginning around the age of three. Repeat your explanation periodically (every week or so). Your explanation may not carry much weight until the child reaches the age of around five, though. If you can, use visual aides to display the consequences of not keeping the body clean and teeth and hair brushed.

- During the first six years of life, rely on Building 95% of the time by using positive, loving or playful ways of leading the child into the hygienic activity.

- As a last resort, for children around three and over, use your Negative Consequence Option *correctly* (without anger or stress) to motivate your child's cooperation. Warn the child of the privilege that not washing will cost her and follow through if necessary.

- For children under three, offer the child two chances to cooperate. Then, calmly and quickly wash the child without criticizing or complaining, even as the child cries. If this displeases her, and it probably will, explain that if she cooperates and washes herself you will not have to do this.

Solution 10:
Toilet Training

Some parents get their children out of diapers and onto a toilet as young as eighteen months old. Ask them how they do it and they will say, "The child just cooperated." It's like early use of the toilet is a gift some children are born with. For the smoothest journey to the toilet for your youngster, consider the following.

- The more anxious you feel about your child's potty training, the more difficult it will be for her to live up to your hopes. Do not worry that your child will not be potty trained in time for pre-school. Your insecurity influences her to act in line with your negative expectations. Maintaining a totally confident attitude helps the child fulfill your highest expectations. Begin visualizing and anticipating your child's potty training success from day one.
- Let your child see you using the toilet and let her join you in the bathroom while you use it. Based on The Law Of Reflection, this plants the seed that will motivate her to use the toilet as soon as she can.
- When your child shows resistance to using the toilet, take it totally in stride, confident that he will succeed in this area.
- When he does use the toilet, show your pleasure. Cheer his accomplishment. But don't go overboard or he may learn to resist using the toilet for manipulation purposes.
- When he has "an accident" have him join you in the cleanup, but do not treat this as punishment. Remain compassionate, calm and confident.
- Until he tells you that he needs to go to the bathroom, invite him to go there on a timed basis, based on your observation of bladder and bowel rhythms as well as his "I need to go" body

language (touching himself, pressing his legs together, and squirming are common indicators).

- If your child refuses to go to the bathroom when you ask, try using a Building method (a loving or playful way of leading him where you want him to go). If that fails, ask no more than once more. Then wait about five or ten minutes before asking again.

If your child does not demonstrate sufficient potty training to be admitted into preschool, consider and eradicate these factors that typically contribute to the delay:

- You express too much emotional intensity regarding the issue.
- The child feels overly controlled and opposed in other areas, and this represents one area where he can assert his self-will.
- Too much change, instability or unhappiness has been going on in the household.
- A new child who is not potty trained has arrived, and that new arrival seems to get all of the attention.
- There may be a physical reason requiring medical investigation and treatment.

Solution 11:
Pacifiers / Thumb Sucking

If you can avoid introducing a pacifier, do so. But remember that your child's nerves, and your nerves, need some soothing for wellbeing for both of you and for your child's development. Purists would disagree with me, but I regard permitting the child's temporary and minimal use of a pacifier as acceptable for the sake of more important factors. (By "minimal" I mean as little as possible without producing excessive emotional upset to the child or to the household at large.) End use of the pacifier no later than by the age of four.

- As her fourth birthday approaches, discuss the fact that there will be no more pacifiers because four-year-olds don't use them.
- Once your child reaches four, explain to him the possible damage done to his teeth caused by continued use of pacifiers. Even show him pictures of terribly decayed and deformed teeth and say, "This is what can happen if you continue using a pacifier beyond the age of four." Many children will elect to stop then and there. Simply remove the pacifier from that point forward.
- Don't be surprised if this causes her sleep habits and bedtime behavior to regress for a while. Things will normalize in about ninety days if you remain kind but consistent.
- Your child may begin chewing on his shirt as a substitute to help him to relax. Be patient with this behavior. Reacting too sternly or with anger or stress increases the stress your child feels.

Thumb Sucking

Thumb sucking presents a somewhat more complicated problem because you cannot remove the child's thumbs! If your child shows a tendency toward thumb sucking beyond the first six months of life, you may want to introduce a pacifier to help her break that habit, because you *can* remove the pacifier later. Other ways to deal with the problem include:

- If it is too late for a pacifier, provide your child with all of the elements discussed in this book that promote positive behavior, feelings of security, and higher development.
- Thumb sucking may be a reflection of someone in the child's environment who demonstrates an oral fixation of some sort, including an obsessive over-eater. Until you improve the surrounding influences, you make it harder to improve the child's behavior.
- Definitely do not use negative emotion or critical speech to motivate your child to do better. That would only drive her deeper into regressive behavior.
- Make your child feel emotionally safe to express herself. A child may thumb suck to keep herself from talking if her parents have made her afraid to say the "wrong" thing.
- Use Building to help your child break the thumb sucking habit by getting your child to, say, join you in song, which would require her to take her thumb out of her mouth.
- Since thumb sucking usually takes place during idle time, permit no TV watching or passive video viewing as soon as the thumb goes in the mouth (or do this as a Negative Consequence following the second warning).
- Try using Negative Consequences in a broader way by letting your child know (from the age of 3 years) that thumb sucking at any time will warrant a warning. After the second warning, a Negative Consequence will be imposed. Do this only once a day or you make it too hard on your child.
- Consult your pediatrician and the Internet, as there are always new inventions coming to the child's rescue in this area.

Solution 12:
Public Behavior

The rules for public behavior depend basically upon the protocol of each particular location, be it your place of worship, the grocery store, a formal restaurant, the library, or Grandma's. When your child's behavior oversteps the boundaries of a particular location's propriety, you need to step in, not just to teach your child appropriate self-conduct, but out of respect for the people present and maybe for the place itself. To do so, try the following:

- A change in environment or routine often triggers some level of regression in children under six, as you learned in the solution relating to transitions. Therefore, when out with your under six child, be prepared to provide her with more focused engagement than usual to help her keep her behavior on track.

- For a child over the age of three, verbally inform the child of the behavior you want and gently remind him of it on the way to the location. Try to create a picture in the child's mind of the correct way to behave. Say little or nothing about the behavior you do *not* want, or you plant the idea of behaving *that* way in his mind.

- By the time your child reaches the age of four, you can explain before arriving that if he behaves *properly* in the location, you will bring him along more often. Otherwise, he will be left home (with a sitter).

- For children older than five, be willing to explain why a particular location calls for particular behavior. For instance, you might explain, "In church, people want quiet surroundings to pray deeply. If a child's behavior distracts them, it makes it harder for them to do that."

- Present children under the age of six with practical demonstrations and exercises at home that give them practice in behaving appropriately in places you plan to take them. For instance, you might say, "This is how we sit in church." Then you might sit upright, with your hands in your lap, in silence.
- Before you go to a more restrictive location, give your child some freedom to satisfy his desire for intense, unhindered activity. This may help him to settle into an orderly mode afterwards.
- If possible, bring things for the child under six to quietly play with that help him to remain occupied and settled down.
- Bring snacks, even to a restaurant, to prevent him from getting too hungry. If food is not permitted in the location, try to have him well fed beforehand.
- Once in the location, maintain your peace and poise. If you become nervous, uptight, agitated, or even excited, you run the risk of inciting your child's unruly behavior.
- If you see the signs of beginning restlessness in your child, you might try taking him outside for a while, or to another part of the location, where he may enjoy more freedom, at least for a while.
- If your child begins to act out, do not use angry, stressful threats, criticism or complaining to control her behavior. While this may produce a superficial semblance of temporary improvement, it teaches the child poor relationship skills, makes both parent and child unhappy, and turns the experience into a negative drain, all of which lead to more child behavior problems later.
- Discipline *yourself* not to stress out worrying about what other people may be thinking about your parenting or your child. Concentrate on making the best decisions you can make from a basic state of calm confidence and self-respect.
- When your child oversteps his boundaries, try some calm Conscious Detachment, but if he begins annoying others, you need to quickly intervene.
- When intervention becomes necessary, first try a Building

(Child-Discipline Option 3) approach by engaging with him more closely, in a loving way, to help him keep his behavior on track. You might play a quiet game with him. This approach helps him to feel loved by you and important to you, which may be exactly what he needs to demonstrate finer behavior.

- If Building does not work, or if it seems inappropriate or unfeasible, for children four and older you might try warning of Negative Consequences by saying something like, "If you continue running in the library, there will be no playground afterwards." If that fails to produce immediate results, though, you have no choice but to remove your child from that location as quickly and quietly as possible.

- For a child too out of control or too young (under four) to be influenced by a warning of a Negative Consequence, calmly and briskly remove the child from that location. If it is a place the child likes and wants to be in, he will relate with the removal as a Negative Consequence. In that event, explain to him how he needs to behave to be permitted to return.

- If the child of three or under does not want to be in that location, accept that this child cannot responsibly handle being in that location at this time. Don't blame the child or complain about it. Accept her limitations patiently, and creatively work around them. Do not repeatedly place your child in situations where he experiences failure, or you undermine his self-confidence and you allow poor behavioral habits to develop.

- If your child is too big to carry and refuses to leave, maintain your composure and accept the limitation of your power for now. Remain calm and wait for your opportunity to restore order or to gain control without anger and with a minimum of strife or commotion. Later, you can talk about what happened and decide if the situation warrants a Negative Consequence. If so, you might say something like, "Because you carried on in the grocery store like that, shouting at me and calling me names, you lose your privilege to play with your new train set for a while." However, in conversation, you may discover something going on in the child's life that deeply troubles her and needs to be addressed. For instance, perhaps she has been witnessing too much ugly fighting going on in your marriage, and she was merely repeating behavior that has been modeled.

Solution 13:
Cleanup Time

Orderly, tidy environments help one to feel and to do one's best. Regard leading your child into cleaning up his room and cleaning up after himself—not as something he does for you, but rather as a discipline and skill he needs to develop *for himself.* Developing the habit of cleaning up her own room and cleaning up after herself helps her to become self-sufficient and successful. You can explain this to children six years old and up.

Any person, be it child or adult, who lives in disorder cannot feel or do his best. Therefore, if your child refuses to cleanup, consider occasionally doing it for him. Don't see this as a favor, but as a way of providing essential support to his wellbeing and development.

There is nothing wrong with a child occasionally creating a big mess, for that can relieve tension and give her some healthy, creative self-expression and exercise.

Freedom to create a big mess, though, needs to be balanced by the child's exercise of the skills and self-discipline needed to create or restore order. In fact, allowing a child to create massive disarray, and then having the child restore order (with your assistance as needed), teaches the child some valuable lessons, including:

- Creating a big mess means a lot of work afterwards.
- This is how we create a big mess.
- This is how to restore order to a big mess.
- The same basic steps involved in cleaning a messy room can be followed to clear up a messy situation in life.
- You don't have to feel afraid or overwhelmed by the sight of a big mess.
- You *can* bring order to large fields of chaos (builds self-confidence).
- To help a child age five and up access the self-motivation needed to cleanup, discuss these lessons with him.
- Cultivate your child's natural desire and ability to create order

by providing her with stable, harmonious, orderly surroundings. Chaotic, contentious, disruptive, messy surroundings and
situations bring out messy child behavior. If you react with
much anger and stress, the chaotic emotional atmosphere you
generate makes the child feel emotionally "messed up" and
drives him to "mess up." Practice handling any mess your child
makes in a calm, confident, orderly manner.

- By the age of three have your child making her bed, tidying up
  her room, and cleaning up after herself in general, on a routine
  basis. Give her all the help and involvement she needs from you
  but gradually turn these chores over to her more and more.

- Engage your child in cleanup without anger or stress.
  Otherwise, your expression of frustration, impatience or annoyance triggers the child's defensive urge to resist more strongly,
  meaning that you basically undermine your objectives.

If your child refuses or ignores you when you verbally request
or direct her to clean up, repeat yourself no more than one time. If
the second verbal attempt fails, you need to consider your Child-
Discipline Options:

- Conscious Detachment: let it go for now and cut her (and yourself) some slack.

- Guiding Choices: try offering a choice you can live with, such
  as, "Do you want to put your red truck away first or your blue
  truck away first?"

- Building (employ this 95% of the time when you choose to take
  action): use a positive, loving, or even playful approach to get
  her involved, such as joining her in the work in a loving, harmonious way; making a game out of it; or singing a song as she
  does the work or you do the work together.

- Negative Consequences: warn her of the privilege loss that will
  follow if she does not fulfill this responsibility. For instance, you
  might say, "If you do not put away your marble run, I will put

it away and you will not be able to use it for a while." Or, "until you clean up your room, you are not going to use an iPod." Employ this option no more than 5% of the time.

For children under six, you can use another approach: Demonstration. Simply do the cleanup in a pleasant fashion in front of your child as she watches you. This encourages her to clean up based on the fact that children under six feel instinctively driven to repeat what they observe others doing.

When your child refuses to clean up, you do not necessary need to do anything about it *right now*. Give yourself all the time you need to calmly consider your Options. In the meantime, you might simply clean up the mess yourself (without hostility or resentment) to create an environment of order that supports the child's positive behavior and development. Don't worry that this may teach him that it is okay to leave a mess. Sometimes, it *is* okay. Sometimes preserving peace and harmony in the home, a loving, harmonious relationship with your child, and an orderly environment around your child is the best you can do to promote your child's best display of orderly, considerate, cooperative behavior.

Solution 14:
Phone Interruptions

In many households, the moment a parent begins talking on the telephone, the child aggressively strives to dominate the parent's attention and tries to get that parent off the phone. Why? It may be simply for the comfort of feeling in control and knowing that the parent is available.

While it can feel particularly annoying to have to deal with your child's domineering tactics when you want or need to focus on a phone conversation, engaging in angry, stressful conflict with your child is no way to solve the problem. By undermining your child's healthy self-respect as well as your own and damaging the relationship between you, fighting with a child leads the child into more combative, not more cooperative behavior.

If your child has demonstrated a pattern of competing with the phone for your attention, the first rule is, when you really do need to have an important conversation, do your best to schedule it when your child is not around. Of course, this is not always possible. There are many things you can do, however, to minimize your child's phone call interference and improve their respectful cooperation. Consider the following solutions:

- For children age three and up, offer a simple, brief description of the rules of courtesy that pertain when someone is on the phone:
  - "You remain quiet around the person on the phone.
  - "You interrupt only when you absolutely have to.
  - "You get the person's attention by politely saying, 'Excuse me.' Then you give the person a moment to break away."
  - Deliver this message during a peaceful time, when you are *not* on the phone.
- Model the behavior you want. Consistently avoid interrupting

others around your child and, when you need to interrupt, do
so politely.

- For children under the age of six, harness the child's instinctive
  drive to repeat behavior she observes by providing demonstra-
  tion-lessons of phone courtesy. For example, when you are not
  actually on the phone, hold a phone to your ear and say to your
  child, as well as to a few dolls, stuffed animals, or even some toy
  cars, something like, "Now everyone, while someone is on the
  phone, we remain quiet and we do not interrupt. We wait
  patiently until the call is over and we hear the person say,
  'Goodbye'." Follow that explanation with a pretend phone conversation lasting about 15 seconds. Then, thank them for their
  cooperation. Repeat this once; then give your child a turn to be
  on the phone while you demonstrate this quiet way of cooper-
  ating. Be prepared to repeat this performance from time to time
  during the child's first six years of life.

- While you are on the phone, be alert enough to notice when
  your child uses the polite form of interrupting. If you do not
  respond when she seeks your attention in an appropriate fashion, you encourage her to use aggressive, intrusive tactics to
  reach you.

- Realize that *how* you speak on the phone impacts your child.
  Speaking with intensity around a child triggers the child's
  aggression and insecurity, driving him to impatiently demand
  control. Speak in calm, gentle tones around the child, maintaining your peaceful center of self-control.

- When your child interrupts, preserve your peace and poise. If
  you seem at all annoyed, you incite more domineering behavior
  from him.

- Realize that your child may in fact require and deserve more of
  your involvement when she wants it, meaning that now may
  not be a good time for you to focus on the phone. Don't presume that just because you have to take or to make a phone call

that your child "should" cooperate. When children interfere with our agenda it often expresses a legitimate need. If this is the case, end the call and give your child your involvement.

- For children under six, demonstrate some extra flexibility while on the phone. Be willing to remain involved with your child during the call. You might give her little challenges like, "Let's see if you can run to your room, touch something blue, and then come back," to buy yourself some time. Sometimes, just holding and snuggling the child while you calmly converse over the phone is enough.

- If you feel the need to focus more completely on the phone call, try carrying on the conversation while ignoring your child's efforts to dominate your attention. By simply not giving him your attention, you avoid rewarding his efforts and thereby reinforcing them. Employing this tactic represents a use of your Conscious Detachment Option.

- A more assertive use of Conscious Detachment would involve a logistical change. Can you walk out of the room with the phone in hand, creating enough distance so that your child's noisy efforts to dominate your attention neither disturb nor distract you?

- One Building tactic that works well with some children between eighteen months and four years of age entails giving the child a play phone to use while you speak on the phone. Since children at that age feel driven to do as you do, the child may imitate your gestures and sounds and carry out her own imaginary conversation while you are on your phone call.

- If that does not work, you can use your option of Guiding Choices. To do this, you might say, "Would you like to color quietly as I complete this call or quietly build with your blocks for a few minutes?"

- If Guiding Choices fails, consider either ending the phone call for now, or moving on to your Negative Consequence Option, using the 1-2-3 Warning System. To employ this Option, you

might say something like, "Please remain quiet so I can complete this call. If you continue banging on the table to get my
attention, the consequence will be that we will not go to the pond
to feed the ducks as we planned to do when I am done." Give her
no more than two warnings. If her behavior does not improve
after that, she gets the consequence. However, be prepared for the
very real possibility that this may not end her disruptive behavior
then and there, so you might still need to cut your call short. If
that becomes necessary, remain calm and do not engage in chastising, criticizing or complaining. Trust that your child gave you
the best she had to give at that time. Engage with her in a loving
way and give the consequence a chance to deliver the lesson that
if she expects you to cooperate with what she wants to do, she will
have to cooperate with what you want to do.

- For children small enough to carry, you may try the UNtimed-out
  Option as described in the chapter on Negative Consequences. To
  employ this, you might warn, "If you continue screaming at me
  to get off the phone, I will take you to your room." Repeat this
  warning one time. If the behavior does not sufficiently improve,
  follow through. But do not lock the door or demand that he
  remain there for any length of time. Simply walk away and see
  what happens. If he returns to you, act as if nothing has happened.
  If he resumes his domineering tactic to get you off the phone, you
  might repeat this procedure. It may, ultimately, turn into a sort of
  game, which can be okay, if it permits you to complete your call,
  albeit with some interruption, while preserving a harmonious, loving relationship with your child.

- For children older than six, if the child wants to say something
  to you or ask you a question, pause in your phone call to
  respectfully hear what your child has to say. Remain calm, flexible, and patient. If he interrupts repeatedly, consider the possibility that now may not actually be a good time for you to focus
  on this call. If that is not the case, patiently ask for some time

to finish the call. Your fair, considerate, calm response will generally elicit considerate, respectful cooperation from your child. If you express much impatience or annoyance in reaction to the interruption, you risk needlessly antagonizing him into the use of even more aggressive control and manipulation tactics, as your hostile reaction models that sort of response for him, makes your relationship with him more contentious, and the atmosphere of discord and disdain lowers his morale.

Solution 15:
Behavior Challenges While You Drive

When children behave in disturbing ways while you drive, the situation can get explosive because you may feel trapped in a moving car. The preservation of your peace and poise becomes of the utmost importance and the family's physical safety depends upon it.

For children three years and older, prior to a car trip, describe proper car behavior and explain the safety reasons behind it. You don't have to go through your entire explanation before every trip, but remind the child of it often enough to keep it fresh in his mind.

For children between three and six years of age, present the child with play-demonstrations of appropriate car behavior. You might involve the child's dolls or stuffed animals as you pretend to drive a make-believe car. Have the demonstration last no longer than your child's patience or your child may grow restless. Having him experience sitting quietly and behaving well in a make-believe car even for a short time can help him replicate that behavior in a real car during much longer periods and it will make your verbal reminders while in the car more influential.

For the sake of their contentment as well as for their most complete development, children under the age of six in particular require an abundance of freedom of bodily movement. Before deciding to bring your child in the car with you for an errand that you need to run, consider the possibility that you may better serve your child, and yourself, by being be more creative in your scheduling to avoid forcing your child to spend more time than necessary in a car.

When your child's car behavior starts to tax you, consider the possibility that he just may need a break from the captivity of the car. In that case, patiently maintain your peace and poise and pull off the road at your next best opportunity to let him have some free time.

In particular, children under six require nearly constant, constructive activity outlets for their development and to make them feel content. Be sure to have toys, books, or games your child can work with.

Keep to an absolute minimum reliance on TV or DVD viewing (in the car or elsewhere), for passive viewing of this nature produces a distracted, numb and unfocused mind, particularly detrimental in the foundation plane of development (occurring in the first six years). It also promotes escapism while dulling creativity and diminishing responsible self-motivation. Time in the car presents an opportunity for family bonding and nurturing engagement, as well as for your child's direct observation of the world in which she lives. Accept the challenge to your own and to your child's creativity to make the time spent in the car constructive and harmonious. To keep younger children calm and content in the car, have snacks and drinks available.

When your child engages in behavior that you find challenging while you drive, remain committed to preserving your calm self-control as your number one priority. This not only constitutes the safest way of dealing with what happens on the road, it avoids increasing the commotion in the car with a stressful reaction.

Particularly when you feel strained, the sound of your critical or correcting voice might incite even more disturbing conduct from a child. Therefore, don't *automatically* issue verbal directions or commands to gain control. Sometimes, bearing with the child's antics as silently and as serenely as possible for a short while works best as the child settles down on his own.

While you may prefer to direct your attention elsewhere, while driving with an unruly child in the car, you may need to focus enough attention on the child in order to preserve enough order to drive safely. If calmly enduring your child's behavior (your Conscious Detachment Option) does not work or seems too passive, *95% of the time* your best option involves providing the child with more loving involvement (your Building Option). You might do this by engaging your child in pleasant conversation, in a song or in a game like spotting specific colors of cars or trucks while on the road.

As a last resort for children around three and older, you may encourage the child to exercise better self-control in the car by warning of a Negative Consequence that you will impose immediately, or at some later time, in or out of the car. For instance, you might warn, "If you continue spitting at your brother we will not be stopping for an ice cream on the way home." If you are headed someplace that your child wants to go, as soon as possible, you may warn them that you will pull off the road and remain stopped for a while if the behavior does not improve.

If nothing you try impacts your child's behavior positively, you may have no choice but to exercise *your* best self-control and endure the situation safely and sanely or perhaps try positive forms of engagement again. If things get so out-of-hand that you begin losing your self-control, pull off the road as soon as you can to give *yourself* a cool-down period.

Solution 16
Encouraging Honesty

No one can lead a child to be more honest than they are themselves. Yet, adults typically seem inclined to react harshly to a child's fabrications, as if a stern response will create a perfectly honest human being. The fact is that out of weakness all humans lie, but we also want to know and tell the truth. Be honest with your child about honesty. Scientists, philosophers and even historians agree that the exact truth lies beyond what human ability can report. Don't present yourself as perfectly honest or you teach your child, by your false example, to lie even more. By doing your best to consistently live your life and relate with your child in a loving, authentic manner, you lead your child to be about as honest as you are.

Children naturally love to know what is really going on and to report on it. They also love fantastic stories. Lead your child toward honesty in a way that carefully avoids stifling her budding creative imagination. Encourage honesty *and* imaginativeness, for together those forces comprise problem-solving ability—the ability to face facts accurately, imagine possibilities, and believe in what *may* be. Imagination provides endless means for effectively expressing and dealing with what is. If your child tells you a tall tale, don't jump to the conclusion that she wants to mislead you, she may actually be trying to interest and entertain you and exercise her imaginative abilities. In that case, play along. For instance, your child might say, "Today an elephant ate the teacher." You might respond, "That's nice, honey. I think I ate that elephant for lunch."

Rarely do we demonstrate enough *self*-honesty to admit how we contribute to our children's departures from the truth by modeling falseness. Every time you try to appear to someone as someone you are not, make a false statement to win an argument, exaggerate in any way, your example influences children to mislead. Some parents seem more concerned with making their children present a public image of the perfect family than with relating with deep, genuine kindness and consideration with one another behind closed doors. Your child will exhibit about as much honesty as you do. If you feel concerned about your child's dishonesty, try being more honest yourself and particularly more honest *with* yourself.

Recognizing your weaknesses in the area of honesty will help you to be more compassionate and understanding when your child misrepresents facts. This in, and of itself, encourages the child to be more open and honest with you.

All human beings make mistakes and give a disappointing performance at times, including children, *and no amount of harshness in your reactions will change that fact.* Children begin lying to their parents when they stop trusting their parents with the truth. A parent's unrealistic expectations and emotional instability encourages a child to instinctively say what he thinks the parent wants to hear. Encouraging your child's honesty involves dealing with a child's inevitable missteps and weaknesses in a way that insures that the child feels safe, both physically and emotionally, to open up to you and expose his authentic self.

Pay close attention to your child's feelings during all of your interactions with her. Consistently relate with her in a way that allows her to feel comfortable being herself with you.

When your child tells you something that you know to be untrue, do not automatically react with anger or stress and definitely do not call the child a "liar" or begin relating to him as a dishonest person because:

- Your negative labels work as self-fulfilling prophesies.
- If you react strongly over his dishonesty, you make him feel a sense of power that encourages him to use dishonesty for power in the future.
- You discourage honesty when you react in a harsh manner that

hurts the child's feelings because this arouses his natural defensiveness which lends itself to falsification, not openness.

You teach your child to be as honest as he can by perceiving and responding to reality as well as you can. When your child gives you a false report, calmly and patiently consider her reason or motivation. A lie often has complicated roots that you need to patiently address.

She may be expressing a need for you to show more compassionate understanding in order for her to feel safe to open up to you.

She may be using the best verbal skills she has to tell you something. For instance, a four-year old might say, "I don't like Jessie anymore," when what she is really saying is, "Do you think Jessie still likes me?" In a case like this, what may first look like a manipulative lie may actually be the child's best stab at expressing the truth, calling for your acceptance and appreciation as her best effort to be open and honest with you. Consider these other possibilities:

- He may be trying to protect someone and that seems more important than telling the truth.
- Perhaps he saw no really good option for dealing with his problem.
- He may actually believe that you will not love him or that it would cause you too much pain if you knew the truth.

Do not attempt to encourage honesty with a show of disapproval or disappointment when your child displays deceit, as those sorts of responses incite further defensiveness and manipulation. Consistently relate to your child as an honest, honorable person to cultivate her honorable self-image, because children choose behaviors that conform to their self-image.

If you doubt your child's story, don't interrogate in an aggressive or threatening manner that will incite the child's distrust in you. Let the matter go and either wait for the facts to emerge on their own or seek them out on your own.

If your child tells you an untruth as an underhanded means of getting something she wants from you, like, "Mommy said it is okay for me to have ice cream today," respond in a calm, compassionate way (to preserve her trust) as you deal with the facts appropriately. If you know that what she has told you is not true, you can state that fact, but don't argue about it. Simply deny the request. Thus, by not giving her the result she is after you discourage her from using the tactic.

If your child repeatedly relies on deception to manipulate, someone has no doubt been modeling it for her. While it may help to have a loving, harmonious discussion (not a lecture) about honesty and its values, and dishonesty and its dangers, you need to improve the behavioral influences surrounding her to improve her behavior.

When your child tells you the truth about a mistake she made or a rule she broke, respond with great pleasure over her courage and honesty. While she may need to come up with a way to rectify the situation (like giving back something she stole), no additional Negative Consequences need to be imposed. If no rectification is possible, you can require some form of community service or have them assist an injured individual. For instance, because she broke her mother's high-heeled shoe while playing with it, she needs to help her mother out with a chore, write a sincere note of apology or draw her mother a picture—whatever way of improving things seems appropriate to the child's stage of development. If the child feels the pain of regret over her actions, just allowing her to feel the pain of regret (without you adding to it with chastising) may be a totally adequate response from you by permitting her to learn from the Natural Consequence of her deed.

By the time your child reaches five years old, engage in discussions in which you explain the role that honesty plays in both their personal and professional life. Tell your child of four or older the story of "The Boy Who Cried Wolf."

Solution 17:
School Related Behavior

Children, like all healthy adults, love to succeed. They love to demonstrate excellence and to be recognized for it. They love to learn. In other words, your child is naturally driven from within toward school success. Presume, therefore, that your child wants to do well in school and that if her behavior or performance flounders, it disturbs her at least as much as it disturbs you, even if she claims that she doesn't care. To support your child's higher potential for school success:

- Consistently relate with your child in a loving way that demonstrates confidence in him. Don't use a withdrawal of your love, respect, inclusion, or approval to motivate higher performance because that tactic produces the opposite effect.

- If your child exhibits a behavior problem at school (or daycare), or shows a lack of self-discipline and motivation regarding schoolwork, look for the root causes first in his home life. While there may be a problem with, say, the way his teacher relates to him, very often a child's troubling behavior outside the home reflects a condition inside the home. Perhaps his mother causes him to feel that she cares more about his scholastic achievement than she cares about him. Perhaps his parents have been bickering with one another to the extent that he feels anxious about it. Perhaps a parent or sibling displays a hostile attitude toward education, school or authority. As you improve a child's home life experience, you support his higher school performance.

- Be aware of the attitude you express toward your child's teacher. If she hears you sounding hostile, condescending or critical toward her teacher, your child may act out that attitude in school through some form of disrespectful behavior.

The quality of the child's school behavior may decline when the child goes through major change or upheaval in his life (see Solution 1). If your child contends with this issue:

- Demonstrate more tolerance and compassionate understanding and do not demand his highest level of school performance at this time.
- Inform his teacher of the situation (you do not have to get too personal or specific) and request that she relate with your child with more patience, compassion and tolerance during this period.
- Be patient. It can take months of normalcy for a child to readjust to his situation.

One of the most common causes of a child's school behavior problem can be traced to forcing the child to remain separated from a parent for too long. Regard the following as general guidelines for the ideal schedule for a child.

- Children under the age of three do best spending their typical day with a parent.
- If you cannot provide your child with all your full-time presence, it is often preferable to have the child remain at home with a loving family member or nanny rather than to sending him to another location.
- During the first three years, a loving in-home, day-care setting that caters to a low number of children is often preferable to a larger, more commercial site.
- From three to six years of age, the child is ready to spend a half-day (from about 9 a.m. till noon or 1 p.m.) five days a week in a preschool environment that provides structured developmental activities and socialization. Beginning at the age of four, if the child is comfortable with it, extend his stay up till 3 p.m. Maintain this routine through the summer. This consistency supports the child's sense of stability.
- From six years of age on, have the child return home from school to a parent.

Note: *If you cannot match these ideals, come as close to them as possible and make the time you spend with your child as harmonious and loving as possible. At the same time, relentlessly seek creative ways to arrange your life so as to provide your child with as much of your time that will benefit her.*

If you receive a complaint from school regarding your child's performance or behavior, don't institute Negative Consequences at home. Let your child's school experience provide her with the Natural Consequences of her actions. And don't use expressions of displeasure or disapproval to lead your child to do her best, as this would invariably function counter to your objective. If your child is over five years of age, she may be able to help you understand what she needs by verbalizing her problem, prompted by your gentle inquiry as to what might be bothering her. In any event, work at improving the quality of your connection with your child. At the same time, you may need to establish more structure at home (rules of responsible conduct backed up by the correct application of your Negative Consequence Option) to help her develop better self-discipline.

Sometimes all the child needs is some tutorial assistance to strengthen his academic skills. Provide this without relating with the child in a way that makes him see himself as a failure or as a disappointment. If he refuses to work with a tutor, use your Negative Consequence Option to provide him with added incentive. For instance, he loses TV privileges or the privilege of riding his bike until he willingly works with the tutor. If this does not work, something deeper is troubling her and you need to find out what that is and address it.

From six years of age, regard your child's schoolwork as her job of preparation for supporting herself in the world. Thus, hold your child accountable for school performance by treating her grades and work habits as a sort of currency for her privileges. Establish the rule that she needs to maintain excellent grades (no less than A's and B's) or to at least exhibit what you regard as totally responsible, excellent work habits, in order to preserve all of the privileges you would otherwise allow her. Let the time of privilege restriction last until the next report card or until you see her work habits show enough improvement for one month. If her grades go down or her work-habits slacken, resume the privilege restriction. Explain to your child that you are doing this to orient her to the real world of personal responsibility.

Don't be "a parent dropout." A child is more likely to drop out of school or lose interest in his schoolwork when his parents "drop out" of their child's school experience. Stay involved by going to parent-teacher conferences, staying familiar with what your child is learning, being aware of homework assignments and school projects. Routinely talk with your child about his school experience (from the age of five years old and up). Don't expect your three year old to have much to say about his school experience that makes any sense to you.

Sometimes the child's school behavior problem has to do with something going wrong at school. Observe your child closely when she comes home from school. If she seems unhappy, more aggressive, or anxious, there may be something happening at school that you need to deal with. If your child is five or older, you may learn about the problem by gently discussing it with him but a meeting with the teacher will most likely prove necessary. Meet with the teacher to discuss how she relates with him, and offer any advice that you might have regarding ways of relating with your child that work at home. When discussing your concerns with your child's teacher:

- Relate with the teacher as a necessary teammate, not as an opponent. Converse in a calm, kind, respectful manner, careful not to needlessly trigger the teacher's defensiveness.
- If things do not improve after the meeting, attend your child's class to observe the teacher at work.
- If that does not solve the problem, or if you cannot do that,

meet with the person in charge of the teacher (the school principal or preschool director) to discuss your concerns.

- If the situation does not improve after that, meet with the teacher and/or principal (director) regularly to continue working on getting everyone as constructively engaged as possible in line with your child's interests.

Homework

Homework is to be done 5 days (or evenings) a week. When your child does not have a homework assignment from school, establish the rule that during homework time she must do some sort of studying or exercise aimed at developing her academic skills and knowledge. Have her produce work for extra credit.

Establish a set time and place in the home where homework is to be done. Allow your child to choose when and where in the home he does his homework. However, let him know that he needs to demonstrate consistent academic success to preserve this privilege, otherwise, you will determine the place and time he does his homework and he will have to stick with that until his grades show sufficient improvement.

Let her know that she is responsible for starting her homework on time. As the time for homework advances, inform her that you will remind her no more than a couple of times, unless she asks you not to. After the time for homework arrives and she has not started on her own, remind her a couple of times. If she neglects to start her homework on time and work all the way through the designated period, or does not produce what you regard as satisfactory work, institute your Negative Consequence Option.

If your child wants your assistance or company, be available. However, offer no more assistance than necessary but coach her along in an encouraging way. Do not use expressions of impatience, annoyance or frustration with your child. This undermines rather than supports higher performance and causes the child to feel more resistant toward schoolwork.

If, while you assist or join your child, he becomes frustrated or begins relating to you disrespectfully out of impatience, remain calm. Kindly let him know that you will not continue helping him unless he maintains his composure and treats you with respect. The following solutions will assist in a successful homework session:

- Make it a household rule applying to siblings that during any child's homework time, the home remains quiet and calm and the one doing homework remains undisturbed.
- Do not permit TV viewing during homework. If your child wants to listen to quiet music, allow it; but he must demonstrate consistent academic success to preserve that privilege.
- Do not permit your child to receive or to make social phone calls or emails during homework time.
- If your child wants to do homework with a friend or at a friend's house, allow that only as long as she demonstrates the level of responsibility to be entrusted with that privilege.

Bullying

The child who bullies at school most likely witnesses or feels like the victim of a bully at home. Consistently model compassionate, respectful relating toward and around your child to avoid or solve this problem.

Consistently demonstrate unconditional love and acceptance toward your child to insure that she feels comfortable sharing with you the humiliating fact that she is being bullied at school if that is indeed going on. If you become aware that your child is being bullied:

- Record the incident in writing and maintain a written report of such incidents as you learn about them.
- Advise your child to stay away from the bully and help her to understand what might be going on in the bully's life that may cause her to pick on other children. This helps your child to not

take the bully's actions personally.
- *Immediately* inform the teacher and principal.
- If the bullying continues, make it clear to the school that you hold the school 100% legally responsible for any bullying or other forms of abuse that occurs there.
- Demand a school policy be instituted (and upheld) involving suspension for the first and second bullying offense and expulsion for the third offense—with immediate expulsion for causing physical injury or serious endangerment.
- If things do not improve, report the pattern and most recent incident to the police and remove your child from that school if necessary. There is no need for you to confront the bully's parents directly, and good reason not to, as that may serve to escalate your problems.

Solution 18:
Chores

Children in the first six years of life naturally want to do what they see being done around them, to join you in whatever you happen to be doing around them, and to feel a sense of contribution. During this period they are, therefore, naturally poised to begin developing the discipline and skills involved in the performance of household chores. This is the time, then, to invite and welcome your child into helping out around the house.

Have a child-sized broom, carpet sweeper, and mop available for your toddler (they love them as gifts), and give your child her own set of rags and a spray bottle. When she attempts to perform a chore out, be very encouraging, even if it slows you down. Don't make her feel wrong or inadequate for doing an imperfect job. The more she feels a sense of accomplishment and contribution in connection with chores now, the more motivated she will feel to help out in later developmental stages.

From the age of six on, assign to your child two household chores a day beyond his responsibility for taking care of his own things, cleaning up after himself, and keeping his room in order.

Explain to your child of six years and older the reason you want him to do chores. Your explanation might run something like this: "As you create order and care for our home, you develop the discipline and skills to manage your environments. A clean, organized environment helps people to feel good and to perform at their highest level, earning them the privileges they want and the ability to do their best for others."

From the age of six years of age, have a weekly or monthly family meeting about chores in which:

- You agree with your child on the chores your child has responsibility for doing.

- You explain that you will remind him no more than two times when his time for doing a chore has arrived. After the second reminder, if he has not taken care of the chore, you will impose a Negative Consequence.
- Your child can change his chores if he likes. If you have more than one child, the children can rotate their chores.
- Explain that in addition to the scheduled chores, you will expect cooperation with your occasional, spontaneous request for your assistance, like answering the door while you are on the phone or helping you carry groceries in from the car.

When you encounter resistance from your child toward doing a chore or picking up after herself, resort to your Building Child-Discipline Option the vast majority of the time by employing a loving or even playful way of leading the child into action. For instance, you might offer to make her bed with her rather than sternly demanding that she do it on her own; or you might turn the process of picking up toys strewn upon the floor into a game or into a dance as you sing.

If the Building Option does not work after two tries, or if you deem it too soft, introduce the Negative Consequence Option by connecting the executing of the chore with a privilege she enjoys. If the chore is not done, the privilege is suspended for a time.

If you use the Negative Consequence Option, offer your child an explanation as to why, when all is calm between you (not in the heat of a conflict). You might say something like, "In life, if you keep a messy, dirty, disorganized environment you function at a lower level and produce poorer results. In your job, this would mean you make less money, so you could not buy things like bicycles and TV sets and even cell phones. Therefore, to prepare you to handle this reality of life, we connect your performing at least two household chores, plus keeping your room clean and neat, with your privileges."

If your child accepts the Negative Consequence rather than

doing the chore, deal with that gracefully. Find another way to get the chore done if it needs to get done. In the meantime, give the consequence a chance to work. If things don't improve, look for the cause in the child's surroundings and in the way you relate with him. Here, as in all other areas of child behavior, a stable, harmonious household and a close, secure relationship with you serve as foundations for your child's responsible self-direction.

Solution 19:
Allowance

Giving a child an allowance gives her practice in money management. You may begin giving your child an allowance as soon as she exhibits the capacity to understand and appreciate receiving money; but get started no later than by the age of six. Make it an amount you consider to be a responsible sum of money for that child to receive, within the limits of your budget,

From the age of six on, offer your child an explanation of the purpose behind your giving an allowance, expressing it along these lines: "Our purpose in giving you an allowance is to help you to develop an understanding of how money works. Your allowance is yours to spend on items or activities that we approve of. You can save it up for important purchases or spend it quickly on pointless ones. Ten percent of the money you earn must be placed in a savings account that you cannot touch until you reach adulthood or unless some need arises where the family must go into it. This is to instill in you the habit of saving. The more you save, the more you let your money work for you."

As your child's savings grow, explore with her the opportunities for saving and investment that will yield her higher interest. You want your child to enter adulthood fully informed about responsible money management.

Establish the fact that allowance is earned, not given. It can be diminished or entirely withheld as a consequence for not fulfilling responsibilities, just as adults may lose income for irresponsible conduct relative to their jobs.

• If your child wants to make a purchase that you regard as irresponsible, tell him that you will offer him no more than two warnings.

- If he insists on following through with the purchase, allow that, and do not rescue him by paying for his mistake.

Regarding Credit Cards: Do not provide your child with one. For college age children living away from home, provide a debit card that cannot be used beyond the limit in the checking account to which it is attached. If you continue to provide your college age child with an allowance, make weekly deposits into the checking account, rather than monthly, to keep a lid on possible impulse spending.

Solution 20:
Pets

When my son Gabriel was a toddler it would not be unusual to see him with his tongue hanging out. I attributed this to the fact that he spent the first years of his life surrounded by our three large, often panting dogs. The principle that children under the age of six naturally become like those they spend time with applies to animals in their surroundings as well as to people. Thus, a child under six who spends much time with an aggressive animal develops aggressiveness. Expose a child to dogs who bark loudly on a routine basis and the child will very likely create loud bursts of noise when she feels excited.

Here are some other things to keep in mind when you consider bringing a pet into your home, or if you already have one. Before you bring a pet home, be sure it will have the environment, attention and general care it needs to be happy, at peace, and healthy. A happy, healthy, relaxed pet in the house contributes feelings of peace and contentment to the home atmosphere, which supports the child's positive behavior, mood and attitude. However, an unhappy, poorly cared for pet exudes stress that fuels household strife.

Based on the Law of Reflection:

How you behave toward an animal teaches your child to behave similarly. If you harshly reprimand or strike an animal, for instance, your child learns to lash out similarly, and not just at animals.

On the flip side, if you consistently treat your pet with tender loving care and respect, your child learns that loving mode of relating. The natural sweetness and innocence expressed by the pet fosters and reinforces the child's sweet, natural innocence. The loving devotion and loyalty that a pet exhibits cultivates the child's capacity to demonstrate the virtues of loving devotion and loyalty.

A loving pet in the home provides the child with companionship and a larger sense of family. It also emotionally nurtures the child with the love and devotion directed toward the child from the pet.

Having a pet in the home gives the child the opportunity to develop a sense of responsibility and the capability to care for others. Involve your child in the care of the pet consistent with the degree of the child's ability. Even your eighteen month old can help you feed a pet, fill the bowl with water, brush or walk the pet. From the age of six on, give your child some definite responsibility for taking care of the pet and treat that as one of the child's chores (see Solution 18).

If your child under the age of six exhibits physically rough treatment of the pet, maintain your compassionate attitude toward *both* your child and the pet, but physically intervene to protect the pet and to establish appropriate behavioral boundaries for your child.

- If you react with anger or stress, you model *in*sensitivity, not sensitivity. Additionally, you cause the child to regard the pet as competition for your affection, which would prompt the child toward even more aggressive treatment of the animal.

- For children under the age of six, immediately after intervening, physically demonstrate the kind way of physically relating with the animal.

- If the child's behavior does not improve, time *the pet out* to a safe location in which the pet can feel comfortable. You want to always demonstrate that you care first and foremost for your child, even as you demonstrate loving care for the pet.

- If your child continues mistreating the pet, it often indicates that the child is being exposed to too much intense aggression in his surroundings, or is being treated too firmly and insensitively. Make adjustments to the child's surroundings in line with the behavior you want from your child.

- When children six and older mistreat an animal, regard it as a symptom of a serious issue that your child feels deeply disturbed about. Pay close attention and engage in gentle inquiry with your child to discover and address the problem. If things don't improve, seek professional assistance to get the bottom of the cause.

- In the event that your child's pet dies, regard that as an opportunity to begin your child's preparation for coming to terms with life and love and death and for getting through those inevitable bouts with painful loss that life has in store. Treat the matter with solemnity. Have some kind of ceremony to help the child move through the deeper meaning of the experience. Definitely let him know that it is okay to grieve, that grieving is nothing to be afraid of and that grieving is a healthy expression of love.

Solution 21:
Music Practice, Art, Sports, Hobbies

A child's engagement in the likes of music, art, mechanics, sports, cheerleading, school politics, community service, and hobbies of craft and collectables advances his overall development, self-discipline, and education. Even reading comic books cultivates a passion for reading and the skills of concentration and comprehension, and it can translate into improved writing and artistic skill.

A child's passion for learning about great sports heroes leads him to develop study habits and to emulate the virtues of championship. As she masters a new karate or dance move, she develops self-confidence, persistence and problem-solving ability. As he plays well with his teammates on the volleyball court, he develops interpersonal skills that can help him to get along better and to work better with others. As she works on her stamp collection she cultivates her ability to handle fine details and learns how to organize.

Of course, you have responsibility for prohibiting your child's involvement in a harmful or degrading interest, one that would lead him on a path of disrespect for self, for others, for other living creatures, for the environment. As your child applies himself to any healthy interest, though, he develops skills and knowledge that can be translated to other areas of achievement, including school and later, to livelihood. As she excels and demonstrates greater mastery in any area, she gains the subconscious education of how to excel and develop mastery in all other areas.

Encourage your child to be the best she can be in the area of her interest, but do not push her to do better or to develop further or faster than her interest-level, otherwise, your pushiness may backfire, causing her to reject her own natural interest because of the unnatural way you insist that she follow it.

Your child's true passion points the way to her genuine happiness and success. Trying to impose your interest on your child, or trying to suppress your child's natural interest because you don't share it, is the equivalent of attempting to steal a child's happiness and best chance for success, because your child can only do and feel his best in life by doing what he most enjoys.

As your child explores his interests, he grows more attuned to what he really wants to do with his life, to his true calling, to his true friends, to his true *self*. When you treat your child's interest with respect, you help your child to feel self-respect.

By showing interest in your child's interest, you help your child to take her interests seriously enough to pursue them with intent. When a parent shows apathy to a child's interests, the child feels less motivated in general to fully apply himself to goals and accomplishments.

If your child is, say, a natural artist or athlete, her engagement in that field may satisfy a deep emotional need, the overlooking of which may have been prompting a behavior problem.

When a natural artist, craftsperson, athlete, or politician connects with his area of interest, he feels more motivated to lead a self-disciplined lifestyle to fulfill his inspiration.

As your child's performance ability develops in his field of interest, it can help him socially. It may even start him on a path that turns into a rewarding and satisfying professional career.

Even if your child expresses no interest in, say, playing a musical instrument, bring musical instruments of all sorts into your child's surroundings, making them available for him to explore even before he is old enough for formal lessons. The mere presence of instruments offers a child a richer cultural experience.

If your child expresses to you that he wants to quit playing a particular instrument, do some gentle inquiry to find out the reason. It may actually be that he loves the instrument but feels embarrassed by his peers' opinion of it. In that event, you might pursue two routes. First, discuss the virtue of courageously following one's true, authentic path even when others mock it. Bring up examples from history of those heroes who went against the current of popular opinion. Second, be willing to cooperate with his sensitivities by helping him to continue his pursuit of his interest in a low profile way until he feels confident enough to be more open.

If your child starts, and then stops practicing due to a genuine loss of interest, don't demand that she stick with it out of fear that she will turn into a quitter. You might gently encourage her to stick with it when her interest wanes, explaining that inspiration levels naturally go up and down and that she may in fact discover this to be a temporary lull in her enthusiasm preceding a major breakthrough in her ability if she works through it. If she lets it go and then later wants to try again, the break may have taught her about what she really values; in that case, be supportive of her returning.

Finding one's true passion requires some experimentation. If your child genuinely desires to switch to another instrument or hobby, be supportive. If he wants to return to a previous interest, support that as well. He may, in the long run, develop into a more well rounded individual on account of his varied experience.

If your child does not keep up his practice because he has lost motivation or has become distracted by (or more interested in) other things, inform him that you will stop paying for lessons if he does not keep up his practice. If that does not improve his practice habits, accept the situation and be pleased about the positive experience, however short-lived, he has received.

Go to her games or performances; show interest in what she has built or drawn or collected; be her encouraging cheerleader, even during her practice sessions. Thus, you build a sacred bond between you and your child. As you support what your child loves, you demonstrate your love for your child.

Solution 22:
TV, Music, Video Games, The Internet

Sensational video images that flash rapidly and strikingly on the child's optic nerve, aimed at overriding the child's control over his attention, over-stimulate the child, making her more aggressive and chaotic and rendering her less able to control her behavior and focus their attention.

Expose a child to sounds and scenes of a violent, base, or crude nature and that child will feel driven to act out similarly. Even funny, furry, friendly "monsters" on an educational kid's show teach the child to contort their faces ghoulishly and to mimic similarly loony antics. Think of the sounds, sights and activities that engage your child as seeds of your child's future forms of self-expression. Every lewd Internet image, violent lyric, and bloody video game battle that gets your child's attention also gets your child in the sense that it programs your child to copy what he receives. The younger the child, the deeper and stronger the programming. You don't need a certified scientific study to verify any of this. Simply observe your child closely, persistently and self-honestly to recognize that what goes in does indeed, come out.

Closely monitor what your child views, listens to, and plays with. Provide your child with the highest cultural influences possible, including masterpieces of sound and sight and the sublime influences of nature. Expose her as little as possible to sounds and images that you do not want her to play back in the forms of her own self-expression.

Absolutely avoid disturbing or frightening children under the age of six years-old with harsh or threatening sounds and sights as this not only causes them severe pain, it disrupts the development of their finer sensibilities.

Simply do not permit your child to "feed" on negative, degrading, destructive cultural influences by prohibiting their entry into your home.

Use the Negative Consequence Option to create boundaries in this area. First, establish the rule of what sort of TV, music, video games, and Internet exposure you permit and how much. As a general rule, the less passive viewing of TV images, the better, as child development advances through the child's active engagement and direct experience. The child who breaks the rule loses the privilege of independent engagement in that media for a while.

Be mindful of the fact that what a child selects to listen to, to view and to do expresses how she feels inside. A child drawn to the macabre comes from a situation that he finds emotionally dark and troubling. A child drawn to violence and rage has been conditioned to "feel at home" with those influences. The child who seems passively open to any influence at all has quite likely been exposed to individuals who display extreme apathy. Merely attempting to limit your child's exposure to media through rules and consequences, without addressing the underlying causes that fuel her drives, will prove futile and may even backfire. To have your child make the best media choices for herself and to demonstrate the highest level of cooperation with your judgment in this area, consistently provide your child with:

• Your close, loving, respectful involvement
• A stable and harmonious home-life
• Examples of integrity that she can trust

Solution 23:
Siblings And Friends

While the following focuses primarily on sibling relationships, it can be applied to close friendships as well. Particularly during the first six years of life, siblings and friends have a greater impact on child behavior and development than many realize. Based on The Law Of Reflection, how someone (of any age) behaves around your child, leads your child to behave similarly, but the influences received in the first six years go in the deepest and demonstrate the most persistent effects.

Additionally, what your child repeatedly experiences in a relationship with a sibling or close friend, she will expect to be repeated in future relationships. Thus, if one of your children routinely physically or emotionally hurts or takes advantage of the other in any way, the "victim" child resists future relationships due to low self-confidence (expecting the same result). Also, based on The Law Of Reflection, she learns to mistreat others similarly.

Don't force your children to spend too much time together. Children stop getting along when they need a break from one another. If they begin bickering, try separating them physically for a while, not as a punishment, but for their (and your) relief.

Be prepared to keep a very close watch over children under the age of six, when their social skills are in the most basic stages of formation. They require the most adult involvement and assistance for staying on track.

When children mistreat one another and you deem it necessary to step in, express the attitude of being an advocate of *both* children (or of all the children involved). Avoid making it look or sound like you are taking sides for one against the other.

The vast majority of time, when siblings squabble or carry on in a manner too disturbing for you to tolerate, involve yourself with the children and participate in what they are doing, assuming the role of coach or leader. For instance, if the children fight over a particular toy, you might step in and say, "Okay children, if you want to have this toy, here is how we all will play with it..." then, have them take turns with it. If that doesn't work, see if you can engage them in another game altogether. For instance, you might run with the toy and they have to catch you. Once you defuse their conflict, lead them into an activity that engages them harmoniously.

For children six years of age and older, you can establish the rule that when you observe one person mistreating the other, *for whatever reason,* the one doing the mistreatment receives no more than two warnings (unless the mistreatment is too serious). When you do this, be sure to have a conversation later to help you understand what happened, and to provide your child with an acceptable way of dealing with it.

Keep in mind that sibling rivalry occurs in both obvious and subtle ways. You can recognize it easily when one vocally teases another or when the two fight physically. It becomes more difficult to detect when one child manipulatively charms your attention away from the other or secretly antagonizes the other so that she explodes before your eyes. Once your children reach the stage of ability to communicate with you and one child looks glum, do some gentle verbal inquiry to find out how he feels treated by his sibling.

If you learn that he indeed does feel mistreated by his sibling, promise him that you will do more to insure that he feels safe and cared about. Then, have a talk with the other child to help him to find kinder, more respectful ways of handling his challenges with his sibling. Ask if there is anything you can do to help him in this. He might say that he would like you to be more aware of the ways his sibling mistreats *him.* In that case, agree to do just that.

If a child under six oversteps the physical boundaries of another child, rely more on physical supervision than on verbalizing rules and issuing consequences after the fact. Refer to Solution 7, pertaining to physical aggression.

When siblings conflict, avoid intervening too quickly. Some sibling rivalry actually contributes to child development. As siblings work problems out on their own they learn how to get along and develop skills they can translate into future relationships. Closely observe as you patiently give the children a chance to handle the situation on their own. Automatically jumping into the fray might merely escalate the problem.

While avoiding intervening too quickly, you still have to insure that no child feels over-powered, devalued or in any other way abused by another child. The way the children carry on with one another does not cause people around them to feel disrespected and mistreated. When you observe any of this going on:

- Intervene at once, but maintain your peace and poise.
- If you react with a show of anger, stress, anxiety or are overwhelmed, you portray yourself as a victim, inciting the children to ignore your rules and requests and will relate with even less respect toward you and others.

For children around the age of six and up, if they routinely mistreat one another, have a family meeting in which you write out a list of the rules of appropriate relating, backed up by the Negative Consequence Option. For instance, your list might include, "Not using your siblings belongings without your sibling's permission." If a child breaks this rule, you can issue one or two warnings that a Negative Consequence will follow. If your child repeats the behavior following the second warning, follow through on administering your Negative Consequence to that child.

Sharing

In the first six years of life, a child is developing the sense of ownership. If you force a child to give up what he has, he may not develop an adequate sense of how to care for, preserve and protect what belongs to him. When your child resists sharing, remain calm and sensitive to his feelings. You want him to share, not because he feels forced to, but because he feels *safe* to.

When a child chooses to *not* share, rather than reacting with frustration (which only incites more withholding from the child anyway):

• You might engage the children in a game with an object so that the one in first possession of it sees that it can be fun to share and feels secure enough to do so.

• You might encourage your child to share by saying something like, "You remember how nice it feels when someone lets you play with what they have. How about giving your brother (or friend) that nice feeling now?"

If your child still refuses to share, you might try focusing your attention on the child who feels left out or deprived and engage with that child in a way that helps him to feel cared about. The other child, upon seeing this, may then want to join in and feel inclined to share as a way of forging the connection. Thus, the children learn sharing as a way of connecting with others.

Do not permit a child of any age to grab or take things the other has or owns without asking for it (again, refer to the Solution 7 on physical aggression). If one child asks another for something that child has, and the possessor refuses, the child who made the request must live with that and honor the other child's right of ownership.

When it comes to community property, or something that both children own, establish the rules of taking turns or simply playing with it fairly and not fighting over it. If the children cannot share the item well, they both lose the privilege of playing with or using it for a while. If one complains, explain that you are giving them both the responsibility for interacting together well.

Reporting Or "Tattling"

You want your children to tell you if a sibling's (or friend's) behavior crosses the line of safe or appropriate boundaries, but you do not want your child to tattle as a means gaining a dominant position or using you as a weapon. Therefore, when one child tells on the other:

- Maintain your peace and poise.
- Unless you regard the situation as urgent, say something like, "Thank you very much for the information. I really do want you to report to me if you see your brother doing something he shouldn't."
- From there, consider your Child Discipline Options. In most cases, you might simply go and observe the children a while to see what is going on.
- If you feel certain that your child did what has been reported, and if your regard the behavior as serious enough to warrant action on your part, consider your Child-Discipline Options as explained in the previous part of this book.
- Let the child who did the reporting know that if she feels mistreated, she needs to stop playing with him for a while. Also, express your appreciation for her not following his lead into inappropriate behavior.
- If the reporter ("tattler") demands that you do something, calmly assure her that you will handle it. If she presses on in an effort to control you, consider your Child Discipline Options regarding *that* behavior.

Friends

Regarding your child's friends, you need to know who they are and how your child and her friends treat one another. Have them over your home and observe what occurs.

If your child of any age receives unkind treatment from other children, you need to protect your child from that treatment by disallowing her to spend unsupervised time with them. Keep in mind, though, that children gravitate toward others who treat them unkindly when they receive or perceive unkind treatment demonstrated at home.

The best way to insure that your child forms the finest friendships is to establish the most loving, respectful relationship possible with your child. Demonstrate often the most loving, respectful ways of relating around your child.

If your child seems shy or withdrawn, does not make friends easily or seems easily hurt by feelings of rejection:

- Help your child feel more confident and sure of himself by showing him an abundance of acceptance, approval and appreciation.

- Let him know that being shy or sensitive is totally okay and that he should do what feels right to him and not be concerned with appearing to be popular.

- Avoid pressuring him to fit in or to make friends or criticizing him for being shy, as this just contributes to his lack of self-confidence.

PART SIX

SECONDARY PARENTING SOLUTIONS

Solution 24:
Foster And Adoptive Parenting

Everything you have learned about parenting in this book applies to foster and adoptive parenting, but a few additional points deserve some special attention:

- The arrival of a new child into your home, for whom you have parental responsibility, is bound to be *extremely* challenging for you at times.
- Don't expect the child to do all of the adapting.
- Be prepared to grow more flexible, trusting, competent and creative. Maintaining a close, positive relationship with a child may prove to be the most demanding part of your life.
- Don't be surprised if you find yourself experiencing a strange mix of feelings, including guilt and insecurity over not being the biological parent. You can gradually resolve these, though, by concentrating on being the very best parent you can be.
- Don't be afraid to make a deep connection with a foster child, even if you believe her stay to be temporary. The love you give her will remain with her.

Based on The Law Of Reflection, the child will behave in ways that reflect the conditions, behaviors and attitudes he has been exposed to. The longer the period of exposure, the deeper and more lasting the impact. If the child has come from a deeply troublesome environment, it can take a long while for him to adjust. As a general rule, if you remain consistent in your approach, improvements can begin to surface in a few months.

If you already have a child at home, realize that the child you bring into the home will share all of his past influences with your child. Seriously consider this fact beforehand.

Don't expect your foster or adopted child to automatically relate to you as a loving parent while you are still a stranger to her. Empathize with the child's extreme state of emotional vulnerability. She needs to be able to reliably expect that she does not have to be perfect to maintain her place in your home. Give yourself time to get to know the child and give the child time to *learn* to trust you.

The child may demonstrate difficulty bonding with and trusting others, in reaction to his early, albeit unconscious experience of separation from his biological parents. If this occurs, don't take it personally. Give her time to learn that she can count on others.

Informing The Adopted Child

A child under the age of six will not be able to form a meaningful concept of what it means to be adopted. After that point, discuss the topic in small pieces at a time, constantly assuring the child that there is absolutely no difference in the love between a biological and adoptive parent.

If the child wants to make contact with the biological parents, do not react with a sense of betrayal. Be prepared for this going into the relationship. Be amenable to this (if the biological parents agree). If he merely wants to learn about them, be supportive, but monitor his quest to protect him from any information he may be too young to handle.

Do *not* suggest that he seek out his biological parents or even learn about them. If he feels more secure identifying himself as your child only, support that. However, if the child over the age of six seems disturbed my something mysterious, you may gently inquire if he is interested in learning more about his biological parents, to let him know that it is okay.

Solution 25:
The Marriage Rules

Because children's behaviors, moods and attitudes reflect the quality of their parent's relationship with one another, your marriage skills translate into parenting skills. A strong, harmonious relationship between you and your spouse instills in your child strong emotional security and stability while teaching him relationship skills, not just for now, but for his entire lifetime.

To fully expound upon the principles and practices involved in creating a truly harmonious marriage would require an entire book. I can only sketch out some of the basics here, to give you a sense of the direction to work in.

Once you are married, and particularly when you have a child, the marriage rules in the sense that the quality of your marriage impacts every other area of your life, including your health, your professional life, and your parenting. Therefore, be mindful of the impact of your attitudes, words, thoughts, speech and actions upon the quality of your marriage. Make choices aimed at enhancing and supporting your loving harmony. The loving harmony will enhance and support you.

As you sow in your marriage, so shall you reap in your life. The more kindly, respectfully, and appreciatively you relate with your spouse, the more kindness, respect, and appreciation you will receive in your life. It may not come directly from your spouse, but it will come.

Your results in any area of life depend upon your level of functioning in that area. If you feel dissatisfied with the way your mate relates to you, look for the ways that you need to improve how *you* relate with your mate. As you raise your level of functioning you achieve more satisfying results.

No matter how hard you work at "correcting" your mate, she is only human and therefore must *inevitably* behave in ways that mismatch your desires and expectations. Make it *your* responsibility to learn how to peacefully and happily accept this inevitable fact of life.

If you cannot forgive your mate, do not regard that as your mate's fault. Rather than regarding your mate as not being perfect enough to love, see yourself as not perfect enough to love. Then, work on forgiving yourself for any mistakes you have made. Ultimately, all forgiveness comes down to self-forgiveness.

You bring about what you think about. How you think of your marriage and your mate is not your mate's responsibility. Your mind is a creative instrument that is yours to control. Holding onto negative mental visions of your mate or your marriage will make you feel trapped. Take 100% responsibility for how you think about your mate and marriage. When a thought of your mate or marriage causes you to feel angry or disappointed, realize that it is your thought, and not your mate, that makes you feel that way. Just realizing that you are reacting to a mere thought can help you let it go.

When your mate does something "wrong," or something you dislike or disapprove of, instead of focusing on her error, focus your thought on one or more major mistakes that *you* have made in life, mistakes that cost you thousands of dollars, perhaps, or that hurt others or yourself in some other significant way. Don't do this to beat yourself up, but rather to help you to understand that "to err is human," so you can respond with acceptance, understanding and compassion rather than with resentment.

No one functions at his best in an atmosphere of angry disapproval. For your spouse to give you the best he has to give, concentrate on consistently relating to him a way that expresses your love, trust, confidence and acceptance.

Compassionately responding to your mate's "mistakes" does not mean passively accepting whatever happens. You can help your mate do better, sometimes, by communicating clearly what you want. However, if you feel angry or resentful while communicating your issue, your spouse will most likely respond with defensiveness. To be truly heard, communicate in a manner that expresses your love. Align your word choices, voice tones and body language to convey your loving feelings.

The best way to lead is by example. When your mate relates to you in critical, unloving way, instead of lashing out and reacting in kind, discipline yourself to respond in a way that models how you would prefer to be treated.

Apply the 95/5 Rule. When it comes to your marriage or your mate, permit yourself to think about and to speak about what you do *not* like and what you do *not* want no more than about 5% of the time. The other 95% of the time, think about and speak about what you love, appreciate and admire.

When you feel angry or impatient with your mate, take that as a sign that you have drifted into your own negative emotional pattern that you need to work yourself out of. It may help to just take a break and spend time alone to examine your feelings. Consciously examining your feelings and thoughts will help you realize that you are actually reacting to the past, not to the present, and lead you to peace.

If you have a long-standing pattern of blaming and resenting your mate, you may have to work on freeing yourself from that for a long time, and still only make small degrees of improvement at a time. However, with persistence, you can free yourself (and your mate) from your angry pattern and, as result, enjoy more and more loving peace and harmony in your marriage.

Apply this most important communication key: whenever you feel a sense of struggle, frustration, annoyance or disapproval toward your spouse, whatever you say cannot work. Therefore, before you try to get your point across, establish yourself in feelings of love, respect and confidence or trust.

Don't work overtime on improving problems in your marriage. Be sure that 95% of the time you spend together your main focus is just on getting along and enjoying one another's companionship right now.

Look for ways to be helpful. Be intentional about this. Sometimes you can ask what she wants, but also simply be on the look out for small things you can do to make her life easier or more pleasant. As you do those things you will find yourself feeling happier and with a happier mate.

Identify your spouse's strengths and weaknesses, as well as your own. Then look for ways to rely upon him for the things he is best at, and to have him rely upon you for the things that you are better at.

A peaceful, loving, harmonious relationship depends upon first and foremost on the individuals being at peace, loving and harmonious themselves. Practice being at peace with your mate, particularly when your mate does not seem to be at peace with you. Thus, you avoid letting his stress expand by making you stressful, and you provide him with a peaceful influence that helps him to let go of his stressed out mode.

Maintaining your own peaceful, loving, harmonious state requires an abundance of energy because as fatigue sets in, so does stress and negativity. Be sure to get enough rest, to eat well, exercise enough, and do enough of what inspires you to feel sufficiently energized.

Maintaining a harmonious marriage requires a certain amount of time spent together in harmony. If the marriage begins feeling strained, it may be that you simply need to spend more quality time with one another. Do not regard this as a luxury, but rather as a necessity, because if the marital strain continues it will have a negative impact on every other area of your life, including your health, your parenting and your livelihood.

You also have responsibility for establishing appropriate boundaries in your relationship with your mate. It is okay to say "no" to a request when saying "yes" would cause you to feel overly strained, drained or off the mark of your own true sense of integrity or purpose. You also need to respectfully accept your spouse's "no" for the same reasons.

Solution 26:
Balancing Life

Providing your children with your best parenting requires a true life-balancing act. The fact is, though, that you *can* have a totally satisfying home and family life, the personal experiences you need to fulfill your great potential and sense of purpose, and all the success at work that you want, *while taking excellent care of yourself and your children in the process.*

In fact, you need to have this. As the ancient Greeks said, "Unbalanced forces perish in the void." If you build a house on a foundation out of balance, you can only build it so high before the imbalance at its base causes the entire structure to collapse. This applies to your life. You need to build a life that satisfies the multiplicity of your needs in sufficient measure. Otherwise, the areas of weakness drain the strength out of every other area. In a very real sense, whatever you lose your balance for, you lose.

To help you achieve a balanced life, look over the following points drawn from my *"Balancing Home, Life, and Work Seminar" (available of CD)*:

- Trust that you can treat yourself well and get away with it, because if you do not treat yourself well, you most certainly will *never* get away with *that.*

- Believe that you do not have to live in an overwhelmed and exhausted state. A balanced life can be achieved by you. If you don't believe it, you will give up before you even try.

- Think of yourself as the foundation upon which you build your life. An unbalanced self creates an unbalanced life. Being a balanced self means that you feel good physically and emotionally, that your thinking is clear and focused on positive outcomes, that you expect success, that your heart is open and loving, that you function true to your authentic self, purpose and values. Review Chapter 6, *The G.A.T.E. Of Self-Control* to help you practice handling all things with peace and poise; for this is your key to balanced living.

Create a vision of your life in balance and, on a daily basis, rededicate yourself to finding ways to advance your life in that direction. In your balanced-life vision see and feel yourself:

- Spending enough time with your children and your mate
- Achieving your career and financial goals
- Taking superb physical care of yourself by giving yourself all of the rest and exercise you need
- Enjoying all the great experiences you need to feel fulfilled

Accept the risk. To live in balance you need to give up some control and allow yourself the peace that comes from living in trust, taking the opportunity to appreciate the way things are and taking nothing *too* seriously.

Practice balanced action, doing neither too much nor too little. Don't confuse doing more with accomplishing more. Sometimes, giving yourself a break is just what you need to function at your highest level so that your actions and decisions have the most positive impact.

Provide yourself with the amount of physical exercise you need for health and fitness and the amount of sleep you need to feel wide awake during waking hours. Eat a well-balanced, nutritious diet and avoid over-eating.

Practice mental balance, being neither too positive nor too negative in your thinking. Being overly positive means that you expect your success to come too easily or that irresponsibility has no cost. Being too negative means that you focus too much on what you do not want. You bring about what you think about. Think about what you want to achieve and about what you can do for it rather than worrying about what *might* happen.

Practice balanced communicating. This includes not speaking too much. Talking too much drains energy and breeds confusion. Speak constructively and purposefully. Listen to what *you* say. You talk yourself into what you talk about. Talking too much about what you don't want makes you negative. Also be aware of what you are listening to. What are you being talked into? Listening to too much negativity it will make you negative.

Balance socializing with solitude. Solitude gives you time to sort out your thoughts and feelings, to clarify your deeper values and to learn how to take good care of yourself. Spending too much time alone, however, makes it more difficult to connect naturally with others. Follow your feelings to sense what you need.

Practice spiritual balance. To be balanced at the core of your being, take the risk of living true to your deepest values and honestly examine what you are doing with your life.

Solution 27:
Financial Fitness

If you suffer from financial stress, you in all likelihood lack patience with your children. Financial stress eats away at your morale, energy level, and health, lowering your level of performance in every area of life, and therefore lowering the quality of your results in every area of life. The surprising fact about financial stress is, though, that it has absolutely nothing to do with how much money you make, have, or owe.

Look at the following points drawn from my *Financial Fitness Seminar*™ (AKA: *Out Of Debt, No Sweat: How To Transform Debt Into Wealth*™) for assistance in this important department of life:

- Financial stress is a stressful *reaction* to your financial condition. You can experience as much of it with millions in the bank as with millions in debt. Before you can improve your circumstances, you need to improve your reaction to your circumstances. Another way of stating this principle is: control of your circumstances begins with controlling your reaction to your circumstances. To apply this principle to financial freedom, focus on improving your reaction to your financial situation *before* you attempt to improve your financial situation. Since peace, poise, trust and confidence are healthier conditions than worry, anxiety, stress and feelings of overwhelm, commit to functioning in the former state more consistently, particularly when you think or talk about your financial situation. Recognizing that financial stress is unhealthy, useless, destructive and counterproductive relative to your financial objectives starts you on the road to freedom from financial problems.

- Create a vision of the financial condition you want to be in. Nurture that vision every day by reviewing it. If you find yourself doubting that you can make that vision a reality, reject that thought. Instead of worrying about what you don't want, keep working for what you do want.

- Don't talk about yourself as poor or lacking in opportunity. Keep your mind focused on where you want to end up financially, not on where you do not want to end up.

- Notice how you talk and think about people who have more money than you do. Much of the criticism you hear being said about the rich expresses unconscious jealousy. If you think or speak about wealth in a derogatory manner, you hold yourself back from having it.

- Don't fool yourself into thinking that anyone has the power to make you rich. Accept that the power to prosper is within you, and that your achieving of prosperity depends upon your attitude, your choices and your levels of skill and knowledge. Develop these and you unleash your power to prosper.

- Don't choose a quick and easy buck over integrity. Integrity pays off in the long run. It is an investment in that which lasts.

- Set your own salary. Think about how much you want to be paid for your time and effort and imagine yourself working for that much. No matter how much you actually get paid right now for your work, you are ultimately working to achieve the amount you want to be paid. Remember that.

- Think about what you can do to advance to your financial goal and consistently take whatever steps you can, no matter how small they might seem, to move your life in that direction.

- Being a kind and loving parent and mate has a mysterious connection to success in all areas of life. Strive to be the best parent and marriage partner you can be and your financial fortunes will brighten.

Just as you need to have a few good physical workouts each week for physical fitness, each week, go over your financial situation for *financial fitness*. Get a clear picture of what you are doing with your money and what your money is doing for you. Get clear about what you owe, where your money is going, and where it is coming from. During "workout," try to feel relaxed, comfortable, secure and confident. If you are in debt, spend some time each week learning about debt and how to manage it, as well as researching for the best credit card interest rates. If you have money to save and invest, spend some of this time learning about the best investment and insurance instruments for you. Just as your body would progressively deteriorate from a lack of physical exercise, your financial situation will only get worse if you do not routinely engage in this financial fitness exercise.

Don't imagine that you can ever have so much money that you would not need to exercise skill, efficiency, intelligence and creativity in managing your financial situation. The more you have, the more you have to lose. Whatever your financial situation is presently, as you exercise financial responsibility, you will enjoy the best possible financial conditions.

Solution 28:
Parenting Through Divorce

The grief suffered by the children involved immeasurably compounds the emotional strain and drain experienced by the divorcing parent. As you might reasonably expect, the parent's level of performance declines in virtually every area, including parenting, for the duration of the parent's emotional distress. At the same time, the children involved rely on their parents more then ever for support, as their parents' divorce represents one of the most painful and difficult of transitions life will ever present to them.

Passing through the toughest stages of the divorce as constructively as possible requires a tremendous amount of growth, entailing a very deep and even excruciating journey into self-understanding and transformation. By the end of it, you may feel like a completely new and better person, one wiser, stronger and more compassionate.

To help you provide your child with best possible parental support through the stages of your divorce, do your best to apply the *Parenting With Love* principles and practices presented in this book. Additionally, consider the following pertinent guidelines:

- Review Solution #1, on transitions.
- A divorce can be so emotionally consuming for the divorcing couple that they forget about the children! Remember that children need conscientious parenting through every stage of the divorce.
- The worse you feel, the less you have to give and the worse you make those around you feel. Therefore, regard adequate self-care as the necessary foundation for taking best possible care of your child. For guidance in regaining your own emotional balance see *Solution #26*. Most importantly, get plenty of rest because severe emotional strain drains energy. Additionally, give yourself all of the opportunities you need to vent your own

deepest, darkest feelings without your children being exposed to it.

- When you feel emotionally strained or drained, don't depend upon the children for your support, otherwise you overburden them with emotional responsibility that is not truly theirs. Your role is to be supportive of *them*.

- Inform your child of the impending divorce *only* when you are absolutely certain that you are going through with it. Otherwise, you needlessly cause your child grief.

- If your child appears not to care about the divorce, a state of denial blinds you, your child, or the both of you. You may be so resistant to seeing your child's pain that you convince yourself it is not there. Your child may feel so afraid or angry that she attempts to hide her pain behind a blasé mask. In any case, do not fool yourself into believing that the divorce really is no big deal to her and do not attempt to force or rush your child into accepting the divorce or acknowledging its significance. Give her all the time she needs to come to terms with what is happening to her.

- Your child may insist that the divorce is not immanent or not permanent. If your child seems to cling to this fantasy, you might gently say, "One never really knows what the future may bring, but I certainly believe the marriage is over for good." In other words, be honest, but don't force the issue. She may only be able to handle tiny increments of realization at a time.

- Deep down, your child probably feels at least partly responsible for the break up of the family. Explain to him that the divorce is *not* his fault and be prepared to repeat this message many times. Try to help your child understand that the divorce is really no one's "fault," but rather a result of a mutual decision made in the best interest of every family member. Blaming your mate only fuels family strife and contention, which works counter to your children's best interests.

- If your child demonstrates an unusually high degree of anger (for him) or appears adrift in a morose, pessimistic, unmotivated state, don't blame him for it. With the shattering of his dream for his family, a disastrous disappointment has befallen him, and he needs an abundance of your patience, understanding, love and trust—not pressure or criticism—to support his recovery.

- Be courageous enough to help your child express all of her feelings to you, including the most unpleasant ones. If she does not feel inclined to express herself in words, offer some other mediums, like drawing or dancing. The more pain she gets out of her system, the more peace and healing she lets in.

- Out of respect for your child, relate civilly to your child's other parent. When a child witnesses one parent showing insensitivity or disrespect toward the other, or bad-mouthing the other, the child experiences deep inner conflict and a loss of self-respect.

- Work on releasing any resentment you harbor toward your child's other parent, not only for your child, but also for yourself (which indirectly supports the child). Holding onto blame is a way of not facing one's own responsibility and it prevents one from fully moving on. Concentrate on healing yourself, not hating or hurting your ex.

- Regard your ex as a crucial component of your child's wellbeing. Doing anything to make her life more difficult means that your children have a less capable, positive parent to be there for them.

- If you feel a strong aversion to the way that your ex parents your child while in his care, bring the matter up with him in a private discussion, remaining calm and sensitive to his feelings. But do not expect your ex to parent your way. Each individual brings unique strengths to parenting. Rather than struggling to change or to control your ex, try to blend, balance, and compensate to provide your children with the best you both have to offer.

- Don't enter into petty, destructive rivalry with your ex for the child's affection or sympathy. If your child seems to favor her other parent or appreciate her more than makes you feel comfortable, instead of resenting your child or her other parent, let that motivate you to redouble your efforts to improve your own parenting knowledge and skills. In other words, don't vie for the child's approval through superficial manipulation; strive to be the best parent you can be.

- Do everything within your power to prevent your children from exposure to any further strife between you and your ex. While you cannot entirely control the other person, you do the best you can for your children by not contributing to friction, by practicing the highest level of self-control. Work out ongoing issues with your spouse in private, away from the children.

- Do not be averse to expressing friendliness or even love toward your ex in front of your children, but keep it somewhat impersonal to avoid confusing your children with an inconsistent message.

- Whether you are the custodial or non-custodial parent, be as dependable and provide as much consistency as you can in your relationship with your child. Your child has lost something he has been counting on most deeply. To recover his emotional stability, his sense of security and his confidence he needs to have as much regularity and predictability in his life as possible.

For more guidelines that relate to divorce see the solutions on Single Parenting and Step Parenting.

Solution 29:
Single Parenting

Let's face it: meeting the demands of parenting with even the most helpful of mates sometimes feels like an impossible task. What does that say about the challenge of single parenting? And yet, the greater the challenge, the greater the opportunity for growth, fulfillment and joy. At the same time, no one on earth really has responsibility for doing more than they can, not even single parents. To help you do your best to fulfill the responsibility of single parenting, consider the following guidelines, drawn from my seminar, "*Single Parent Survival, Sanity, and Serenity Skills*"™:

- Do your best to apply the basic *Parenting With Love* principles and practices presented in this book.

- Accept the limits of your capacity. This means doing all you can in peace and poise and straining to do no more than that. Functioning in state of being overwhelmed causes you to dysfunction, making you over-react and under-perform in parenting and in every other important area of your life. When you feel calm and confident, you help your children to feel secure.

- Carefully monitor your self-talk. Telling yourself that what you are doing is not good enough, that you are not getting enough done, that you have more to get done than you can do, debilitates one with enormous and useless emotional strain.

- You need to become a master of time management and energy conservation. You have all the time and energy you need to do what must be done, but none to waste. Take time to clarify your priorities and, throughout the day, be extremely selective as to what you deal with and what you let slide.

- Learn to trust what you cannot control. You really have no sane alternative to this. No matter how hard you drive yourself, you cannot do it all and therefore, you have to learn to trust anyway. If you drive yourself too hard, fatigue and stress will make it impossible to escape feelings of anxiety.

- As your child develops, you can turn over more of the chores involved in keeping up the household. This will not rob him of his childhood; it will make him more mature, capable and responsible.

- However, at no time count on your child for your emotional support or you overburden the child with emotional responsibility not truly his own. Seek emotional support from your peers.

- You need a life! You need the support of friends and you need to explore the potential for a new primary relationship. Don't regard this as selfish. It is part of providing yourself with what you need to give your child the best you've got to give. (Review Solution 26: Balancing Life.)

- While you cannot be both mother and father to your child, you can work on bringing your male and female energies into balance in your parenting. The feminine involves forms of bonding, soothing and nurturing. The masculine involves giving the child independence and responsibility for himself and joining the child in activities. Your work on this balancing act will provide your child with more well rounded parenting as it advances you in fulfilling more of your full potential.

- Help your child to develop at least one mentor-like relationship with an adult of your opposite sex—preferably a family member (if your child's other parent cannot fulfill this role).

- If you have to work full-time and you cannot provide your child with as much parenting as she needs, give her all the time that you *can* give and make that time as loving and wonderful for both of you as possible.

- Because of the additional stress placed upon the child and the adults by the restructuring of the family dynamic, give the child (and yourself) time to adjust to life with a single parent before changing their family again to include a new primary adult. The children will feel and do better and your relationship with your new significant other will have a better chance of working out.

- When you begin a new relationship with a special someone, that person may not understand children, or how to constructively relate with them. Give that person this book to read and talk about the principles and practices it puts forth *before* you introduce him into your children's lives. You may discover your interest in this person waning as you learn about his views relating to children. If the two of you cannot agree on the basics of parenting you are probably not a very good match.

- When it comes to issues of child discipline, that remains entirely your domain of responsibility. However, be open to listening to what your "new person" has to say as he may make useful observations from a more objective vantage point.

- If you have a good relationship with your child, bringing home someone new should not disturb him. In fact, if that new relationship is really good for you, your child will appreciate the happiness it brings out of you.

- If your child expresses much criticism toward your new person, it may very likely be an expression of your child's fear of being abandoned by you now that you have found someone new. Make reasonable efforts to reassure your child and continue to consistently provide your child with the highest quality of parenting with love. If the new relationship is really good for you, it will prove really good for your child, and in time your child will see that.

- If your child genuinely dislikes your new person, listen carefully to your child's concerns. If the new person treats you or your child with disrespect or insensitivity, your child may be the first to recognize it.

- It is possible that you and your child will disagree about the new person. You might regard her as really wonderful and your child may hold an opposite view. Don't force your child to spend any more time than she wants with the new person, but let her know that that may diminish the amount of time that you and your child spend together, *because as a human being you need a primary relationship with someone that you believe is right for you.* When you are with your child and the new person, be sure to remain consciously involved with your child, so she feels part of what is going on.

If your new relationship is progressing toward marriage, refer to Solution 30: Stepparenting.

Solution 30: Stepparenting

Despite the common message delivered by fairy tales, a stepparent *can* be of invaluable support to a child. However, the obstacles that stand in the way of this can seem nearly insurmountable at times. The following guidelines ought to be read by the stepparent, the custodial biological parent, and (if there is one) the non-custodial biological parent. If the non-custodial biological parent has a significant other, that individual should also read them because, although indirectly, he will likely exert some influence on the child as well. In some cases, you might even have an older child read them.

Even though the biological parent has primary responsibility for raising the child, you need to be in essential agreement with the parent regarding an issue as crucial as child-raising *before* stepping into the stepparent's role. If you find your mate's parenting practices unacceptable, that alone can doom your relationship.

The stepparent typically enters the family at a distinct disadvantage, being automatically perceived by the stepchild as an intruder and as a threat to life as she has known it. Often, the stepparent personifies the painful transition that makes the child feel so painfully out of control of his own life. Be prepared to face this and, rather than taking it personally, take it "situationally"—that is, regard it as the child's natural response to her challenging situation. As the situation becomes more tenable for the child, the child will be able to gradually relate with you more and more based on who you really are and how well you actually relate with her.

The stepparent's position is undermined when, out of feelings of jealousy or insecurity, an absent biological parent encourages the child to distrust or disrespect the stepparent. This is tragic because a stepparent can provide invaluable support to the child. If for no other reason than the close proximity between the two, a stepparent significantly impacts the child's quality of life and behavior. The better a child's relationship with her stepparent, the better the child feels and functions.

The non-custodial biological parent can help his child greatly by assuming a helpful role with regard to the relationship between his child and the stepparent. This can be done by:

- Refusing to talk in derogatory ways about the stepparent to the child.
- Making himself available for the child to work out problems she may have with the stepparent.
- Making himself available to the stepparent to help him better understand, relate with and support the child.
- Being supportive of the relationship between his ex and the stepparent, like making himself available to care for the child when that couple has an opportunity for a vacation to rejuvenate their relationship (because a harmonious relationship between the child's parent and stepparent supports the child as well).
- Drop expectations of becoming instantly close or of automatically receiving affection, respect and love from your stepchild, particularly with children over the age of six. Accept the fact that you cannot rush or force a loving relationship with a child. You have to *earn* the love, trust, respect and cooperation of a child through consistently relating well with that child over a long period of time.
- Don't try to "buy" the child's love or approval by putting on a false front. Children see through manipulative tactics and you won't be able to sustain empty pretenses for long. Consistently do what you believe to be in the best interest of the child, even if the child does not appear to appreciate it right away, and you will earn the child's respect, trust and appreciation in the long run. (Review Chapter 5, on Your S.E.A.T. Of Authority.)

- Don't expect the child's non-custodial biological parent to instantly treat you with trust and respect either. You will probably need to move slowly and gently here as the parent may naturally feel insecure and suspicious of you for some time.
- Don't compete with the child's absent biological parent. Just as the child benefits from the parent's support of your relationship with the child, the child benefits from your support of the child's relationship with his natural parents.
- Don't compete with the child for your mate's attention. Be prepared for your mate to feel some guilt about bringing you into the child's life, which may cause her to seem a little distant from you for a while.
- Be prepared for your mate to be very involved with the child during the period of adjustment, to help the child to feel secure.
- Look for ways to help the relationship between your mate and her child, even if it means you spending more time alone than you feel comfortable with. The more harmonious the parent-child relationship, the more harmony you will enjoy in your home.
- Relate kindly and respectfully with your mate, particularly in front of the child. If your stepchild witnesses your mistreatment of his parent, you cause the child a serious emotional disturbance.

A common mistake made by the natural parent in the household is to relate disrespectfully and unkindly toward the stepparent as a way of making the child feel that she is on her child's side. On the contrary, the biological parent in the household needs to be totally committed to relating to the stepparent with the utmost kindness and respect, particularly in front of the child. This not only makes it easier for the child to relate kindly and respectfully toward the stepparent; it fosters household harmony that helps the child to feel and function her best.

Establish the rule that the stepchild must relate with the stepparent in a kind, respectful manner, even if the child dislikes the stepparent (obviously, the parent needs to demonstrate abidance of this rule herself). Explain to the child over the age of six that, while you will never appreciate everything about everyone, our goal as virtuous human beings is to treat everyone with respect and kindness nonetheless.

If you are the biological parent and observe this rule being broken, refer to the Child-Discipline Options and choose the one you deem most appropriate. If this rule is broken outside the notice of the biological parent and you are the stepparent, you basically have three options to choose from:

1. First, consider overlooking it and making no big deal about it as you continue to work on getting along with the child in kind, friendly manner.
2. If things do not improve, do some gentle inquiry (with a child over the age of four) to find out what may be troubling the child that you can help with.
3. If that fails, remain calm and give yourself some space if you can. Later, discuss the problem with your mate. In any event, do not use the holding of a grudge, or a subtle form of unkind retaliation, as a manipulative tactic for improving the situation.

Special Note For Blended Families: Neither demand nor expect the children of blended families to instantly relate as natural siblings toward one another. Establish rules of civility and leave the disciplining primarily up to each child's biological parent. At the same time, though, both parents need to be in essential agreement of the parenting practices being exhibited, as these constitute the quality of influence in the surroundings of all the children.

Solution 31:
Grandparenting (And The Extended Family)

One sad mistake made by grandparents is to undervalue their influence upon the grandchild's life. Love compares to fine wine: it grows richer with age. Grandparents deeply enrich a child's life with the added blessing of their loving involvement. For one thing, because of the increased tolerance that comes with the wisdom of their experience, a grandparent's unconditional adoration contributes to the child's sense of self-worth and self-confidence that can propel the child to achieve greater heights in life.

The following guidelines pertain to the fulfillment of the great potential of grandparental involvement, and they are intended for both the parents and the grandparents to read:

- For the good of the grandchild, consistently relate with your own child with the utmost respect. Otherwise, you undermine the parent's authority and cause the child to feel internally conflicted and insecure, which can only promote more problematic behavior from the child.

- If you disapprove of something your child does, discuss it privately with your child, out of earshot of the grandchild.

- If you observe your child making what you consider as a parent to be a mistake, as long as no real emergency exists, concentrate on maintaining your peace, poise and your patience. If it seems too serious to accept passively, refer to the guideline above.

- Invite the parents to let you know if you relate with their child in a manner they have a problem with. When your grandchild's parent expresses a concern regarding how you relate to the children, as long as the message is presented in a respectful, kind manner out of earshot of the grandchild, listen carefully and think about it seriously.

- Do your best to establish a stable routine for visits. This supports your grandchild's emotional stability.
- Don't confuse the giving of material presents with the infinitely more valuable gift of your loving presence.
- When you visit, treat as your first priority providing the grandchild with the primary focus of your attention and involvement. Merely showing up to be around misses a special opportunity for bonding.
- Parents ought not expect grandparents to function as disciplinarians for the children. The grandparent's primary "job" is to nurture the child with unconditional adoration.
- If your child expresses a dislike for his grandparent, try to find out why and explain the problem to the grandparent, with your recommendations. In the meantime, don't force your child to spend more time with his grandparent than he wants to.
- If your child expresses an aversion to experiencing close physical affection with the grandparent, do not force it. Respect your child's sensitivities and sense of boundaries. If the grandparent attempts to force close physical contact with the grandchild, politely but firmly step in as your child's advocate.
- If a grandparent lives in the parent's home, the parents are to relate with their parent in a loving, respectful way, mindful that they model their way of relating to parents for their children.
- If your child's grandparents involve themselves so intrusively that it interferes with your effectiveness as a parent, of if they treat you in an unkind, condescending or disrespectful way in front of your children, have a respectful conversation with them privately in which you clearly inform them that this will not be tolerated. In other words, warn them that *they* will receive a time out if things don't improve. Be ready to follow through on your warning if they ignore it. If you allow anyone to treat you with disrespect in front of your children, you teach your children to disrespect you.
- If the grandparent provides primary economic support, that in no way "purchases" the right to usurp the parent's role, nor does

it make it acceptable to treat the parent with a lack of respect.

- If the parents and child depend upon the grandparent's economic support to the extent that they must live in the grandparent's home, the owner of the home gets to establish the basic rules of household conduct. This may include the grandparent having at least some responsibility for child discipline.

Special Note On Teen Parenting

When pre-adult children become parents, the grandparents often find themselves forced into the role of parenting the grandchild while continuing to raise their own child. Some general guidelines for this special situation include:

- Because of the child's lack of maturity, the grandparent now has to assume both roles for the grandchild: that of parent and grandparent.

- Instruct your child in the skills of parenting and give her opportunities to practice those skills.

- Do not entirely deprive your child of a personal life, because she needs one for her own continuing development; but her freedom must be someone diminished for her to fulfill the additional responsibility of caring for her child.

Extended Family

Avoid the common mistake of speaking in a critical and condescending way in your child's earshot about absent family members. If your child hears you doing this and then sees you acting in front of that relative as if you have no issues with that person, you confuse your child and teach him to be duplicitous and backbiting.

Feeling part of a big, happy, harmonious family helps a child to feel valued and confident, enlarges the child's happiness and love. Do what you can to provide your children with the opportunity for positive, meaningful relationships with his relatives.

Epilogue
In Charge Now?

Two parents stood in a garden. One looked haggard, overwhelmed, anxious, at her wit's end. The other looked serene, pleased, confident, in love. The child of the first parent ran around the garden kicking up soil and tearing at the flowers. The child of the second parent did the same. From the appearance of the children, neither parent seemed to be in charge. From the appearance of the parents, obviously, the second one appeared to be in control. And she was, at least at a beginning stage.

As you have learned in this book, taking charge in your relationship with your child begins with taking charge of yourself first. Your child's behavior will reflect your own. You have to approach your problems in a calm, confident, loving way to produce the best possible outcomes. As long as you make your reactions dependent upon your child's actions, your child runs the show, and not in a pretty way.

How you think of yourself as a parent influences the way that you parent. Think of yourself as a failure and you block your ability to come up with sound solutions. You need to think of yourself as a success to perform like a success. Don't base your thoughts about your parenting upon your child's behavior; base your thoughts about your parenting upon the kind of parent you wish to be. You bring about what you think about.

The best parenting guidance you have available comes from within. Examine your motives every step of the way. Why are you doing what your child wants? Why are you opposing your child's wishes? If you give into your child because you want your child to like you, you make your parenting about your insecurities, not about your child's best interest. If your motive is just to be liked, do not give in. Let your child feel displeased as you establish a boundary: you are establishing your role as a responsible parent.

If you oppose your child's wishes for no other reason than because you habitually cling to a sense of control, let go of your control and see what happens. The real purpose of your control is to assist the child in functioning in line with the child's best interests, not to make the child compensate for your insecurities.

When you react to your child's behavior with anger and stress, you react destructively, and it is not your child's fault. To be the best parent you can be, maintain your peace and poise and pay close, conscious attention to what goes on between you and your child in the present moment. Look at how your responses impact your child. Be attentive enough to sense your child's feelings. You want to relate with your child in a way that supports her feeling good deep down inside; when a child feels badly she cannot do her best.

For your child to feel good, you need to feel good. When you feel good together, you can more easily and effectively lead your child toward the fulfillment of her glorious potential. The better you connect, the better you direct and correct.

To be in charge right now, relax, trust, pay attention and permit yourself to thoroughly enjoy your sacred opportunity to be with your divine gift of a child.

May your home, and may our world, be blessed with peace and love, and the light of parenting solutions that truly work.

"We do not need to be told whether to be strict or permissive with our children. What we do need is to have respect for their needs, their feelings, and their individuality, as well as for our own."

-Dr. Alice Miller

BOB LANCER

Bob Lancer is the host of a unique parenting radio show, "Bob Lancer's Parenting Solutions," that focuses on the raising of ourselves and our society as well as on the raising of our children. His show has been on the air since 1997 and it currently broadcasts to 35 states, while streaming live over the Internet around the world.

He is the author of numerous books of various genres, including children's books. He has created dozens of recordings on parenting, marriage and the fulfillment of the human potential. His work has been published and produced internationally. Currently, a documentary film about his work with parents in economically disadvantaged situations and other challenging social circumstances is in post-production.

"Bob Lancer's Parenting Solutions" has been featured on network television, in national magazines, in major newspapers and on radio and TV stations internationally.

Bob has been a speaker, seminar leader and consultant on issues relating to his themes since 1980, presenting at national and international conferences, major corporations and for groups, businesses, associations, schools, faith-based organizations as well as a wide variety of other venues. He also presents motivational talks to young people on how to make dreams come true and create a better world.

Bob Lancer is a former schoolteacher who has worked with children of all backgrounds and grade levels. He is a husband and a parent, currently living in Atlanta, Georgia.

He is available to speak at conferences, meetings and functions of all kinds, including fundraising activities.

To fulfill your greater potential...
To fulfill the great potential of your family...

BOB LANCER'S
Motivational Speaking Engagements
Seminars and Workshops
Private Consultations

Inspire your audiences with a message of hope and possibility for every family, child and adult.

Enlighten your audience with insight into how to raise ourselves and our world to raise our children to fulfill their glorious potential.

Invite Bob Lancer to present one of his powerful keynote addresses, workshops, or seminars of varying lengths relating to parenting, marriage, child education, professional childcare and individual development.

Bob Lancer also presents powerful motivational keynotes and seminars on personal and professional development issues, including Stress Management, Work/Life Balance, Positive Communication Skills, Team-Building, Spectacular Goal-Achievement, Decision-Making Mastery, and more.

He is available internationally.

For more information on Bob Lancer,
please visit us online at morepower4you.net

Visit morepower4you.net or gdgpublishing.com/boblancer.php
to schedule your next speaking engagement, seminar, workshop
or consultation as well as a complete list of topics and services.

A Selection of Bob Lancer's Recordings on CD
Approximately 50 minutes in length
For a complete list, visit www.boblancer.com

The Peaceful Parent: This CD reinforces everything you learned in this book. Listen over and over to help you maintain your peace and poise for better handling of every parenting challenge.

Natural Parenting: Understand the cycles of child behavior and how to turn negative, repeating patterns into positive, growing spirals of greater parenting success.

Release Your Child's Greatness Now! Learn how and when to let go, to avoid controlling to much. While children do count on us to set certain limits, they also need us to know when to let go to allow them to flourish on their own.

The Marriage Rules Seminar: Children are profoundly impacted by the quality of their parents' relationship. This CD shows you how to get along with your mate in a way that positively impacts your child and achieves the harmonious, loving relationship you and your mate want.

Speak Up / Listen Up: Learn compassionate, positive communication skills to achieve more kind, respectful cooperation and understanding in your relationship with your child and your mate.

The Life-Direction Process: Learn powerful wisdom-strategies for creating the life you want for your family.

Balancing Home, Life And Work: Learn how to achieve spectacular success at work while taking great care of yourself and enjoying a totally fulfilling home and personal life. It can be done!

Time Mastery: Learn how to accomplish more as you eliminate rush and overwhelm from your daily life.

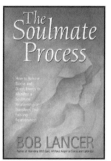